THE POLITE MARRIAGE

THE POLITE MARRIAGE

also

The Didactic Lyre

The Bristol Milkwoman

The Scotch Parents

Clio in Motley

and

Mary Hays, Philosophess

Eighteenth-century essays by

JOYCE MARJORIE SANXTER TOMPKINS

---

*"It is too often forgotten that just as a bad man is
nevertheless a man, so a bad poet is nevertheless a poet"*

G. K. CHESTERTON

Essay Index Reprint Series

BOOKS FOR LIBRARIES PRESS
FREEPORT, NEW YORK

First Published 1938
Reprinted 1969

STANDARD BOOK NUMBER:
8369-1053-2

LIBRARY OF CONGRESS CATALOG CARD NUMBER:
77-80403

PRINTED IN THE UNITED STATES OF AMERICA

To JILL FORSTER BROWN

Dear Jill,

It is with great pleasure that I affix your name to this collection of essays, for I think you understand my care for the small talents and half-smothered voices of the past. You will perhaps remember that all these people, except Dr Downman, made brief appearances in my last book, *The Popular Novel in England* (which you impressed me very much by taking with you into the nursing-home, when you presented me with my niece), but there they were kept strictly subservient to the purposes of literary history. Here they have been allowed to expand their personalities and to display their experiences.

In the small writers the expression of experience is often more direct than in the great. For one thing, the experience is generally more manageable, less complex in its relations with the world of thought and emotion that encloses it. It is therefore less enriched and less altered by the brooding mind, and persists in recognizable shape through many utterances. It retains its personal flavour, especially when, as sometimes happens, it was this experience that first provoked the writer to write. Then, the disguise is of the flimsiest. Secondly, such writers are seldom possessed by any vehement convictions as to the nature of literature or of literary forms. They have taste, not passion. They are not revolutionaries. They accept the literary fashions of their day and shape their material contentedly to them; or they please themselves by mild reforms and small adjustments, which are often singularly indicative

〈 v 〉

of the person behind the book. Where the great writer builds his lofty rhyme, widening his ground-plan and shooting up his pinnacles till the initial experience becomes no more (and no less) than the sacrifice under the threshold, through which the house stands, the small writer constructs a wayside shrine, where through every window we can see the image that it was made to contain.

I hope the eighteenth-century punctuation in the quotations will not worry you. Its significance was largely rhetorical and emotional, not grammatical; it directed the reading voice where to lay the emphasis, and thus preserved the inflection of the sentence as the writer heard it in his own mind. I was very unwilling to obliterate such expressions of temperament as the punctuation of Mary Hays or the author of *The Scotch Parents*. Ann Yearsley's punctuation could well have been normalized; it is quite chaotic in her second book, after Hannah More's elucidating hand had been removed. But I could not well edit her commas and preserve those of Mary Hays; so I have left them all as they were originally placed.

I hope, with some confidence, that you will find pleasure in this book; but the pleasure that comes to me when, from brownish print and yellow pages, I first become aware (sometimes contrary to my expectations) of what was once a living voice, is mine, and it is incommunicable.

Your affectionate sister

J. M. S. TOMPKINS

ROYAL HOLLOWAY COLLEGE
ENGLEFIELD GREEN
31 *January* 1937

CONTENTS

THE POLITE MARRIAGE

ᐱᐱᐱᐱᐱᐱᐱᐱᐱᐱᐱᐱᐱ

1. HENRY AND FRANCES; AN EIGHTEENTH-CENTURY COURTSHIP

ON 19 January 1753, Richard Griffith, farmer and linen manufacturer of Maidenhall, Kilkenny, drew up a will in favour of his young wife, Elizabeth, and her infant son, and, as the marriage was a private one, added on the wrapper of the will an account of his motives in contracting it.

"I was not", he wrote, "over-reached into this Match by Art, nor hurried into it by Passion, but, from long experience of her Sense and Worth, I reasoned myself into it....I found I had so engaged her Affections that no other Man could make her happy; and so dallied with her Character, that only *myself could repair it.*"

The solemn act had induced a mood, not unusual in him, of self-examination, and he noted down the results.

I am in my Religion a Christian; but of the *Arian* Heresy, as it is stiled by bigoted Councils. I was for many years a Deist; till Dr. Clayton, Bishop of Clogher, his Essay on Spirit, and subsequent Writings upon the same Subject, had reconciled the Doctrine of the Trinity to human Reason, and metaphysical science.

> "Humanum est errare et nescire;
> Ens Entium, miserere mei."

This doubtless sincere though something less than passionate petition, copied from the epitaph written by the first Duke of Buckingham for himself, he supplemented with a copy of Pope's *Universal Prayer*, and then sent the whole parcel to the wife whom he dared not yet bring home, to be hoarded with the other testimonies of their troubled courtship—the letters, the poems, the lock of his hair and—perhaps—the locket, discarded gift of a preceding charmer, with which he had so foolishly hoped to propitiate her. Four years later the Griffiths, philosophically content, as they declared, with their very narrow circumstances, but probably a little short of cash, allowed their love-letters to be issued in two volumes as *A Series of Genuine Letters between Henry and Frances*. The genuineness of the letters in the main cannot be doubted. It was accepted by their contemporaries. A few in the second edition were reconstructed from memory, and some may have been worked up into a more systematic form, but they are totally unlike the epistolary fiction of the time; indeed, their very incoherences vouch for them. In the 1760 edition these were to some extent redressed, and the slight disguise of English place-names was dropped, for the authorship was now no secret. The publication of four more volumes, two in 1766 and two in 1770, does not concern us here, for the new letters belong to the later married life of the Griffiths, when she had become the well-known female novelist and translator, for whose *Delicate Distress* Lydia Languish sent to all the circulating libraries in Bath, and he was hoaxing the literary world with his imitations of Sterne. They were still lovers, carrying their wedded happiness with a certain proud consciousness, an ostentation even, overhauling it at times and testifying to its soundness in a bruising world; but this spectacle, admirable as it is, lacks the charm of their early correspondence, where the eternal commonplaces of courtship bloom among outworn modes of thought like familiar flowers in a sampler.

It was on 12 May 1746 that Richard Griffith, hereinafter called Henry, met his fate in the person of Elizabeth Griffith, on whom he presently bestowed the name of Frances. He was then a little over thirty, a masterful and self-sufficient young man, with a broad good-humoured face and a store of miscellaneous reading. She was eleven years younger, small of stature, sensitive and romantic, but with a lively eye and a good deal of coquettish vivacity. Both were of gentle Welsh stock, settled in Ireland, and both were poor, for Frances's father had left her portionless to the guardianship of an old aunt in Abbey Street, Dublin, and Henry, in spite of good connections, had his own way to make. His first thought had been literature, but by now he had burnt his early efforts and was settled with an uncle in the country, where he taught himself French and studied husbandry philosophically, with a view to a farm of his own. Meanwhile his method of life— he was very methodical—did not exclude pleasure, which for him meant "the sweet Indulgence of fond Affections"; and since marriage was out of the question, the solution seemed to lie in a steady, secret and rewarded attachment. One such affair had terminated about a year before he met Frances, and the young man, having found his life a "wretched Vacuum" in the interval, pitched upon her as the next object of his gallantry. The responsive fineness of her nature suited his taste as well as her unprotected situation did his intentions, and by November he had engaged her in a clandestine correspondence with a view to her induction into what was then called the life of honour.

The correspondence alone was a serious matter enough for a girl who had nothing but her reputation, but Frances was adventurous and the rewards were great. They wrote three times a week and met fairly often, when Henry came to visit his friends in Dublin, and from the beginning their correspondence took a wide range. Henry was a resolute self-educator with a bent for speculation, and, fortified by his sympathy, Frances, whose studies had languished since her father's death, turned eagerly back to her books. They discuss music, quote poetry and venture into French; he introduces her to La Rochefoucauld and she makes him respect her enthusiasm for Cowley. He is delighted with her talents; she is his "*dear Sprightly*", his "dearest Sappho, or tenth Muse" (she wrote verse), and later, when they have swept ethics and metaphysics into their net, she is Eloise to his Abelard. What she chiefly sought at this time, one guesses, was companionship, and he, well entertained, could afford to bide his time and conduct his wooing by mannerly degrees; but if Miss Griffith was at any time blind to the reality of the situation, that blindness could not have lasted long. Her letters prickle with oblique remonstrance. She has "a mortal Apprehension that neither my Sense nor Merits can purchase your Esteem, without which your Love would shock me". She plies the advancing lover with definitions of friendship, which he finds "somewhat too abstracted and refined" for him, and turns off with a good-tempered jest. She appeals covertly for mercy on the score of her health, that "fatal Delicacy" of body and spirits which was to form the subject of so many a letter, and for which Henry invariably prescribed a regimen of early hours and regularity. She could never prevail upon herself, however, to follow his advice. She was vivacious and nervous, liked gadding about and disliked paying the price. No doubt her spirits needed stimulus, for she had a difficult part to play. By now her affections were deeply engaged, and she was fighting at once for love and self-respect, with the odds heavily against her. She had to contend with her own quick susceptibilities, vibrating extravagantly under the slightest touch, and with the "provoking, insincere, plausible, philosophick Temper" in which he eluded her attacks. Henry is infinitely adroit, humouring her in a pleasant, elder-brotherly way, and meeting her serious re-proaches in all tones from raillery to manly indignation. "I am sorry you are ill....I am not much better myself....I hope it is owing merely to my Disorder, that your Letter appears very unreasonable and unkind." This brings her to her knees, but she struggles up again, and presently he is promising to wait on her "to talk over your extraordinary and cruel Scheme of banishing me from your Presence for ever". She asks for her letters back and gets instead a lock of his hair; "and, to pay the highest Compliment to female Vanity and Triumph," writes Henry, making a bad mistake for once, "I also send you a Locket, to put it in, which was given me by a very pretty Woman, whose Hair I have taken out and burned this Day in the Midst of some of her Letters, which I had by me". Even in one of her diffident moods, and she was at times painfully diffident, Frances could not pass without rebuke this blot on her lover's "entertaining and improving Correspondence"; he has misunderstood and undervalued her; moreover, she does not approve of his former mistress's taste in lockets.

The climax came when Henry, laying aside coaxing and allusion, presented his demands point-blank. The case was too serious for coquetry, and Frances's answer, grave with its weight of confession and refusal, springs from a valiant heart. In his next appeal Henry tried sophistry. This she found even less tolerable ("it would humour my Pride rather to be over-powered than to be over-reached"), but she followed him into a lighter vein and salted her reply with wit. Nevertheless, he is forbidden on pain of a total breach to reopen the subject. The offending letters, she warns him, have been burnt. "I would have preserved the Wit of them, if I had been Chymist enough to separate the Gold from the Dross; but they perished together in the Flames, the natural Consequence of keeping bad Company."

So they settle down once more to their tormenting, delight-ful converse, but with this difference, that Henry's views and desires undergo a slow reorientation. Early in their acquaint-ance Frances had suggested his writing a novel—advice that he afterwards took. "It would be an easier Task for you than almost any Man," she declared, "for I think your whole Life and Character have a great deal of that Stile in them." The inference was questionable, but Fate underlined the description by casting Henry for that most popular of all roles—the Libertine Reformed. He was to learn from Frances the meaning of the words friendship and love, to read his recantation in letter after letter, and, without finding that his former state called for marked repentance, to rejoice calmly in the new range of sentiment that now lay open to him.

The situation can be matched again and again in the pages of those women writers who were soon almost to appropriate the novel. It was indeed one of their favourite themes. Lady after lady drew her ungrammatical pen to reclaim Lovelace and save Clarissa and to insist, with pathetic ardour, on the ennobling influence of women upon men. But, although these novels are in the epistolary form, they contain no letters like those of Frances. Their heroines uphold a rigid standard of prudence, propriety and female delicacy, and even Frances herself, when she took to novel-writing, punished the smallest indiscretion with an unsparing rod. In life, however, she had dared to steer a dangerous and lonely course; she had injured her fame while refusing to rank herself with women of intrigue and lost her friends without being sure of her lover; she had offended against the holy laws of prudence, and she reaped her reward in jealousy, self-reproach and ecstatic happiness. Small wonder, then, that a living pulse beats in these old letters, and that joy and pain, working on her quick fancy and eager heart, struck forth at times such notes as astonished Henry and still echo plaintively within the covers of the *Genuine Letters*.

Henry wrote her charming compliments on her style and patient remonstrances on her matter. Plagued by her caprice, self-righteously hurt by her recurrent suspicions, but determined to preserve his own constancy and not to lose his pains, he found that his best resource was to take up a packet of her letters, "sometimes more or less", he told his publisher later, "according to the Disorder of my Affection, and so read away till I had swallowed the *quantum sufficit* to restore the full

Health of my Attachment to her....And I have actually, several Times, by mere force of Contemplation, worked myself into such an Enthusiasm about her Knowledge, Genius and Understanding, that, as you will casually observe in going through this Collection, I have wrote *Latin*, Philosophy and Metaphisicks to her, during the Paroxisms of the Fit." We discern here a faintly deprecating note. But if Henry felt that his intellectual intercourse with Frances called for explanation, Frances was in turn elated and oppressed by it. It was a time when formal learning in women was not encouraged, though their lords and masters smiled benignly on the untutored sallies of female genius. The women found themselves, for the most part, forced by their lack of education to fall in with this scheme, and some seem even to have played the role *con amore*, for Henry tells the tale of "a certain Lady, who, upon reading over a Letter, she had wrote about Business, to a Gentleman, and thinking it too Orthographical for a Woman, added an (e) to the Ende of several Wordse, leste it should bee suspected that she had spelte by the Aid of a Dictionarye". But there were others, like Frances, who felt their inferiority with pain and resentment. A teasing allusion of Henry's to the preference of women for fools brings her into the lists as Champion for the Honour of her Injured Sex, referring him in a flurry of argument to history and justice (divine justice, she means) for the "original Excellence of our Natures", and throwing the blame for their deterioration on the "narrow, domestick and partial Education" of women, established in his own interest by the domineering male. Souls, she asserts, have no gender—a point much debated at the time. And have not women been the prime civilizers of man? "All Refinement in Sense, and all Improvement in Manners, was entirely owing to our Influence over your uncooth Natures." Would he, she pertinently asks, enjoy the conversation of a Rabbi, if he had never learnt Hebrew? "Oh! let us once be free!" Henry bows to the storm, admires his Fanny's spirit and throws his palinode at her feet. The civilizing function of women had become a commonplace, together with the superior directness of their understandings, "unincumbered with logical Distinctions", to which he also bears witness; but the concession could not have cost the old Adam in him many pangs, for, apart from the fact that there was no bigotry in his nature, he had other letters of Frances's to which he could turn—tender ecstasies of self-abasement and voluntary dependence on him. "Whatever Sense, Accomplishment, or Merit, I have", she wrote, "were inspired by your Precept, Example and Instruction; and like *Pygmalion*, you are become inamoured with the Works of your own Hands"; and later, "I never take up a Book but with a Design of rendering myself more worthy of your personal and epistolary Converse."

She needed constant reassurance and lived in dread of boring him. When the spirit that inspired her onslaughts flagged, she would recoil and hide herself behind apologies until he soothed her with compliments and enticed her with allusions or, if that would not serve, set her definite tasks to do. Even then she will seldom deal systematically with a subject, but her "slight Touches and irregular Essays", as Henry said, "are like the Tuning of an Instrument by a masterly Hand". She had the quick, bright perceptions which were held to characterize the female genius, a fund of glancing allusions and an easy, sensitive style. Sentences from her letters dwell in the memory with something of the inflection of the spoken word. Friendship, she writes, "is not without its Elations and Transports; the mutual Contemplation of Truth and the Communication of Knowledge being higher Enjoyments than mortal Sense is capable of". The news of an elopement, unsanctioned by marriage, draws from her the comment: "I feel a mortified Pride and Indignation upon all Occasions like this; as I suppose you Men do, when you hear the Story of a Coward; lest it should bring a Reflection upon human Nature in general"; while Henry's delight in his country solitude suggests to her that "we are not only to perfect our-selves in Virtue here, but also in a true Taste and Relish for the Pleasures of the Blest". Henry, trying in vain to lead her into "subjects of some Intricacy and Depth", accused her of cowardice, but her diffidence was only partly temperamental; its main source was her consciousness of standing educationally at a disadvantage, of being precariously upheld by her "kind Preceptor" in an atmosphere too rarefied for her sex to breathe. As a literary critic she has more self-confidence, finds Montaigne much to her taste and follows Henry intrepidly through Tully's *Offices* and Pliny's *Letters* (this last in the translation of John Boyle, Earl of Orrery, husband of Frances's friend and patroness, Lady Orrery). Nor are contemporary letters forgotten, and *Tom Jones* is submitted to Henry for his approval, which, bating the author's ill-judged attempts to be witty ("by no means his Talent") it receives.

Less strenuous letters reflect the circumstances of their daily lives, and we catch a glimpse of Dublin, "not much above ankle-deep in mud", and of Frances, ruined with chair-hires, threatening to print her lover's letters to keep herself in the three necessities of life—tea, clean linen and plays—and signing herself his "affectionate Pauper". Henry writes from Kilkenny Assizes, where he has just watched, for philosophical reasons, the procession of the condemned to the gallows; and, more happily, from a field of barley, where he sits watching the binders and stackers—"forty-seven Women and fourteen Men at Work round about me, while I am reading *Pliny* and writing to you". He sends her pleasant descriptions of his morning walks round the farm—his Ambarvalia he called them. He was a devotee of early rising, finding something in the morning hours that purified his thoughts and strengthened in him that rational and hopeful Deism, which had not yet succumbed to the Arian arguments of the Bishop of Clogher. After his labours there was "a Mutton Chop, a pint of Wine, a Pinch of Snuff, and a Book", and the society of a low-spirited cat who had attached herself to him, and whose "Nerves are so weak (which I attribute to her Drinking Tea in a Morning, without Eating) that the least loud Word sets her trembling; so that I dare not chide an awkward Housemaid, for Fear of putting Madam into her Hysterics".

In this fashion they wove the myriad threads of intimacy and, if Henry was still in ignorance of his Fanny's value, he was to learn it in the most painful and decisive way—by estrangement. For now approaches what they always referred to as the Interregnum in their Loves. Both dreaded lest their relationship should become known, to the detriment of his prospects and her reputation. "My Character is Libertine," he warned her, "your Fortunes are small, your Experience of the World but little, your Age young, your Guardian old." Yet it was Henry's imprudence in showing her letters to a friend that led to the breach. The action came to Frances's ears, and in a spasm of indignation and alarm, she broke with him and demanded her letters back. He sent them with a letter that does him honour, received in return an elaborately polite note of thanks and jumped at the chance of writing again. This time he sent her his portrait, with some poignant remarks on substance and shadow, and followed it up with a case for the portrait, "as it will help to hide even my Shadow from you"; but Frances had been too deeply shaken to come to his lure, and for months the correspondence dropped. Henry pursued his plans for a living with deliberate audacity, taking the lease of 600 acres at Maidenhall, borrowing money and laying out his farms and his linen manufacture. He still met Frances in the houses of mutual friends, and "their behaviour was perfectly well-bred to each other, but a good deal constrained". In his heart he refused to give her up, and at last opportunity rewarded him. One summer afternoon, when he was setting out from Dublin for Kilkenny, he invited three young women of his acquaintance to accompany him as far as Rathcoole and dine there. Frances was included in the invitation and did not refuse. At Rathcoole floods of rain descended, and the party, chaperoned by a matron, sat up all night in the inn, playing cards; and somehow, during those candle-lit, storm-enclosed hours, Henry won to speech with Frances and sealed his peace with her, and the Interregnum was over.

The letters begin again. Henry moves carefully into his stride with delicate gradings of jest and earnest; but Frances's wing is broken. "At last that quick spirit, you have so often complained of, is quite extinct.... Deal plainly with me.... I am weary of this continued Warfare." In answer he commends his love to her, "corrected and amended from the Errors of the former Edition", but refrains from any "particular Declaration" and leaves her heart-sick with the long strain of unsatisfied love. She played for higher stakes than he did, as was inevitable from the nature of the case; but at last Henry's hitherto well-regulated flame is beginning to scorch the edges of his discretion. It was while she was on a visit to Kilkenny, paid ostensibly to his mother and sister, that Henry, walking with her about his own fields, first formed "a sort of vague Determination" to marry her, when his precarious circumstances should permit. He let no word of this escape, however, but with all his usual prudence and an added touch of malice "played back her own Platonicks" and offered her the friendship for which she had once been so earnest an advocate. It no longer sufficed. Poor Frances. She had restored her lover to "the rational Enjoyment of his rural Retreat", as he confesses, with one of his rare admissions of past suffering, but she herself had found no peace there. There were present griefs as well as future uncertainties to trouble her. Her "heart's dear Harry" was taking his incidental pleasures openly, and soon after her return to Dublin she hears that Nancy, supplanted in her master's favour by Sally, has broken out into jealous resentment and been dismissed. She commiserates Nancy; and Henry, aware of a certain tartness in her words, enters on his defence, which puts her in turn to an anxious self-vindication:

As to the affair of *Nancy* and *Sally*, it is of no farther consequence to me, than if *James* and the Coachman had been the Disputants. Nor did I mention my Opinion of Sally with any Design; for you may easily conceive, that it is a matter of Indifference to me, whether your present favourite was christened *Sarah* or *Anne*—for while I am in Possession of the Jewel that is lodged within, I care not who holds the Casket.

> Oh! free, for ever, be his Eye,
> Whose Heart to me is always true.

She could not submit to share the emotions of Nancy, nor could she accuse of infidelity the man who had never pledged himself to her; nevertheless, she does add: "I have quoted these Lines to you before upon some such Occasion", and we hear no more of Henry's amours. Some twenty years later, Frances, in her *History of Lady Barton*, expressed her sense of the case. "There is something extremely indelicate", she writes, "in professing a Passion for a virtuous Woman before we have undergone a sufficient Quarantine after the Contagion of an abandoned one, and Man in such a Situation resembles a Centaur, half human, half brute."

He beat her to the last fort of her pride, and then, as once before, she stood erect and challenged him:

Tell me, my dearest *Harry*, what will all this end in? The little Circle of my Acquaintance speak of my Attachment to you with seeming Pity, from a Belief that you have none to me. The World, in general, treat me in the severest Manner, on your Account. Answer me now, my Heart's dear *Harry*, with Truth and Justice, for Reason prompts the Question and Honour will not dally longer, can you indeed lay your Hand on that dear Breast, where Fanny's Heart inhabits, and tell me you have Love, Honour, and Constancy enough, to repay all her past, present and future Sufferings, by seriously intending, whenever it is in your Power, to make her your Wife?

To the tenderness, the tremulous courage of this address, Henry could make but one reply, but, discreet as usual, he did not make it in writing. There were still obstacles. More than once in the succeeding months Frances's pen sketched an eternal farewell to her lover. But the man who had roused her passions knew how to bear with their fluctuations; and on 12 May 1751, five years after their first meeting, they were married.

It was a private marriage, attended, to safeguard the bride's reputation, by the Countess of Orrery. Henry returned to his farm and his schemes; Frances dwelt with her aunt in Dublin and afterwards in rooms at Chapelizod and elsewhere. Thus they still blacken paper, and Frances still suffers from that complaint so incident to eighteenth-century heroines, aching fingers. Their letters run in a joyous spate of confession and enquiry, for in this secret sunshine Frances recovers her vivacity and becomes once more the "lively, gay, young Love", to whom Henry proposes to send his grey hairs in a locket. Serenity she never achieved; the shadow of a wing falls across all her joys, and Henry is fain to pacify her with an inscription for their tombstone: "*Evasimus! Permutatio felix!*" Meanwhile they run the usual gamut of tenderness according to the fingering of their day, find, with some disquietude, that love makes them disinclined for other company, describe to a hair where they kiss the letters they exchange, and cultivate a fine choice of addresses and of subscriptions. "My dear *Heauton-timorumenos*," writes Henry, and she, mastering enough of the word to serve, signs herself, "Your own *Heautonti*". "I am, my dearest Life," he assures her, "while I have Appetite, Breath or Motion, your own rational Brute." But the prettiest of these terminations belongs to the days of courtship, and Henry prints it entirely in italics:

I am, my dear, little, cross Pett,
your constant, good-humoured, clumsy,
Country Farmer.

Henry's sense of power was sated, and the natural mercifulness of his temper—he warmed flies in his hand in autumn and stayed at a bad inn out of charity—had free play. He cherished his young wife with "one constant, equal Tenderness", and though he still at times acted "the good Farmer's Part" and endeavoured to winnow the chaff of "irregular Whims and romantic Dreams" from her "charming Composition", it was with extreme gentleness. Moreover, he was not backward to avow himself in some things her pupil; she had civilized him, he said; nay, he was more beholden to her than to his mother. "She made me but an Animal; you have made me a Man." This confession redressed the balance between them; the thought of his experience ceased to disquiet her, while her own dependence, instead of galling her pride, became a theme of joy.

She was his friend and his bride, and presently it became clear that she was also the mother of his child. She had met his passion and inspired him with an epithalamium, in which the intended compliment is a little damaged by the exigencies of rhyme.

> Her Air coquettish, but her Mind a Prude,
> Her Body wanton, but her Soul not lewd,

wrote Henry. He was to do better in prose. "My dear little Shrub, my Arbutus, my Evergreen," he salutes her, "I wish you Joy of your Retirement." He sends her a crock of pickled walnuts and promises her a ham. She is to go to bed early, read to employ her mind, and stop "raking"; and: "Remember now, my warmest Wish, that I trust you with yourself." Her pregnancy was painful and exhausting, and in her loneliness her spirits flagged and she became once more, in spite of her struggles, the prey of diffidence and suspicion. "You are either sick, angry or jealous, I observe, once a week," comments Henry and reassures her systematically as to her appearance ("You speak too humbly, my dear Fanny, about

your Person; it is, to my Liking, amiable "), her literary talent
and his enduring affection for her. She certainly felt some
shame to be so captious, but more irritation to see him so self-
possessed. His carefully cherished philosophy was a perpetual
provocation to her, and once, with the remark: "I cannot help
observing with what vast Calmness you have endured my
Misfortunes", she slips past his guard, and has to submit to
one grave rebuke before Henry, pursuing his plan of drawing
her out of herself, passes on to an analysis of Dr Isaac Watts on
Suicide. Frances rallies, promises to take great care of "your
dear little Epitome" and settles down to wait for Henry's
visits, rarer now than before, for he is fifty miles away and
much occupied with his farm. He was not with her on the
day in June 1752 when Richard Griffith, Junior, made his
appearance, and afterwards, when "little *Ourself*" is ill, she
has to sit alone by his cradle, crying and praying. Of his
tenderness for both of them, however, in the depth of her
mind she had no doubt, whatever freaks her fancy might play.

"What sort of a Bab is it?" he enquires solicitously. "Has it
a broad, good-humoured Countenance, like Dad; or a lively Eye,
double Chin, and saucy Look, like Mam? Is it most a Writer or
a Philosopher? Does it incline rather to Poetry or Metaphysics? . . .
In short, tell me every thing about it; what it says, and what it does,
and whether it has ever yet discovered any Ear for Music."

Here we may leave Henry, "exerting all [his] Wit to be a
very great Fool" about his son. The coming years were to test
his fibre. His bold schemes for a livelihood miscarried. He
had received a bounty from Parliament and encouragement to
expect a second and larger one, in anticipation of which he
had completed his works and then mortgaged the whole
property to set the machines in motion. Times had changed
for the worse, however; the bounty was withheld; the inevitable ruin followed, and he was left, "branded with the
title of a Projector", to support a wife and two children,
"without trade, profession, patrimony, or employ; bereft of

all, Hope only remaining in the box". One kind of success still lay open to him, and that he pursued with all the method and tenacity of his nature, taking thought betimes that at least his marriage should not be counted among his misfortunes. His providence was rewarded. In her *Essays addressed to Young Married Women* (1782) Frances looks back on thirty years of happy married life, while Henry, paying her ceremonious compliments on an anniversary of their wedding, foretells with confidence that their loves will hand them down to Fame.

But Fame, having so much weighty lumber to carry, has let the six volumes of the *Genuine Letters* fall, for the *Dictionary of National Biography* to sweep aside with the comment, "A sentimental production". Sentiment there is, both in the modern and the contemporary sense, for these were lovers and writers, who felt and reasoned on their emotions. But there is much more than sentiment; there is passion, humour and a display of character of a kind that English fiction had not yet learned to equal. Indeed, it is strange to see how, in the novels of both Richard and Elizabeth Griffith, autobiographical as they in part are, the fine shades of experience are effaced and the delicate outline blurred by deference to the conventions, literary and moral, of their day. Let the dust on these lie undisturbed, for they hold out no promise; but the adventurous and patient reader who touches the *Genuine Letters* will find that he has life between his hands, and perceive, before he has penetrated very far, a fragrance not wholly faded, a warmth not quite extinct.

2. HENRY AND FRANCES MARRIED

In 1768 Fanny Burney read the *Letters of Henry and Frances*
and liked them prodigiously; she did not know, she
confided to her diary, that she had ever read finer sentiments on piety and Christianity than the second volume
abounded in, and it left her in a grave, sedate mood, unpro-
pitious for the next book she took in hand. This happened to
be *The Vicar of Wakefield*, and the romantic fastidiousness of
Miss Burney's sixteen years was jarred at the outset by the
tone of Dr Primrose's references to his wife, so indifferent, so
contemptuous, as it seemed to her, and so unlike that of Henry
to Frances. The contrast was too severe and she nearly threw
the book aside; and although she persevered and presently had
the gratification of being " *surprised into tears* ", Henry remained
for some time the dominant figure in her imagination. She
dwelt on his style, "so elegantly natural, so tenderly manly,
so unassumingly rational", and longed to read the further
instalment of the *Letters* which, she knew, had been published.
They had increased her relish for *minute, heartfelt* writing;
moreover, they had the supreme charm of the genuine, for
Mr and Mrs Griffith—she had learnt their real names by now
—lived in London, in Hyde Street, Bloomsbury, and cultivated their idyll in the air of the metropolis. They were, as a
matter of fact, acquaintances of the Burneys' old friend,
David Garrick, though Fanny does not seem to have known
this. She burnt her grains of incense in the privacy of her
diary; but the fragrance, had it reached Richard Griffith,
would have gratified him extremely, for she had praised in him
those things which he himself found most worthy of praise, his
elegant Tenderness and fond Affection.

The later letters of Henry and Frances, published in four
volumes between 1766 and 1770, cover about seventeen years
of married life. They are, in their essence, an ode to Hymen,

prolonged through half a generation by two people whose aim, consciously and elaborately pursued, was the stability of their mutual affection, who were convinced that, though love is spontaneous in origin, it is best upheld by calculated policy, and treated their wedded state as a valuable property which it was only common sense to keep in good repair. Every now and then Henry goes over the domestic roof and reports triumphantly that there are no leaks, or Frances compliments her partner on the state of their flower-garden; and then they both walk up and down together and admire their estate, count the years since it was purchased, recall the cost and the improvements they have made, and compare themselves to Hilpa and Shalum, the antediluvian lovers of the *Spectator*.

It is not to be supposed that this parade, with its accompanying ceremonies of compliment and gratulation, was performed wholly without the sense of an audience. By 1766 the Griffiths were fairly widely known as letter writers and as married lovers, and their reputation was a matter of pride to them both. They felt themselves an honour to the human race, and were conscious of a standard to be maintained and of an achievement in the art of living to be discreetly advertised. They had heard their love-letters quoted across the tea-cups by polite guests and found them lying on the window-sills of country houses, and though the effects of this situation need not be measured by the scale of modern publicity, they cannot be ignored. Henry falls into a way of referring to his former letters under their published title—"as I say somewhere in the *Series*"—and she, while maintaining that she wrote without a thought of publication, knew at least that a proud husband was apt to exhibit the sheets. She had protested against the first edition, considering the printing of love-letters almost as indecent as embracing in public, and had specially wished to strike out all "fond Epithets and Passages of Love or Tenderness", but in the end she accepted her role and gave her testimony aloud. A studious care of attitude, a premeditated fulness of expression distinguish these letters from their earlier correspondence. This self-consciousness, however, must not be identified with insincerity. They wrote for each other first and for the world afterwards; for Henry's allusions to his domestic happiness, though he certainly intended them to be overheard, are in the first place tributes to Frances herself, and when he proposes collecting a congregation and reading to them, as First and Second Lessons, the expositions of love in the *Genuine Letters*, the proposal is a jest, but he has no doubt that the letters are gospel. "Are we not the most extraordinary Couple that ever lived?" he asks, and Frances, with her more tremulous accent, cries in passionate reply: "What have twenty years robbed us of?"

As we turn the pages, compliment requites compliment like the bows and curtsies in a minuet. It was a deliberate procedure, a cult of politeness in the most intimate human relationship, as a means of preserving a lively consciousness of each other's value. It was more. There is something hieratic in these postures. They dance before an altar with ritual dignity. And here, before their stateliness stiffens in our fancy to a mechanical drill, we must pause to overcome our distrust of so much explicit virtue, to exorcise, in fact, the petrifying shade of Joseph Surface.

The discrediting of the sententious Joseph has brought suspicion upon all those who practised his art of moral generalization and disposed their virtuous perceptions tastefully in the shop window. It is in the livery of a minor Surface that Henry appears in *Chalmers*; and a generation, which has discarded the urbanities of the eighteenth-century parlour to direct attention to the fellows in the cellarage, will not be very ready to acquit him of disingenuousness or to pass his claim to turn only his best side outward to the world. Yet there is a word to be said for the display of moral sentiment. It was connected both with the artistic ideals of the time and with its social conscience. The citizen of the world, intimately aware of his responsibilities to society, cultivated his virtuous sensations with care, and attempted to crystallize them in words, to ensure their permanency and his power of repeating them. The moments he chose to perpetuate in this way were the high-water marks of his development, the occasions on which he approached most nearly the proper stature of social man. Each moment was an achievement, a contribution to the common stock of right feeling, a subject of decent pride, and as such it was fitting that it should be carefully defined, with all that majestic sententiousness, that polished dignity of explicit statement, which constituted elegance to contemporary taste. But it is the defect of this sort of eloquence that, by engulfing all personal inflections in its rotund utterance, it leaves too little distinction to modern ears between the moral sentiments of Henry and those of Joseph Surface. The moralist is, in consequence, exposed to the charge either of insincerity or of ostentation. Henry has little to fear on the first count, and he would not have been abashed by the second. When he, a man of narrow and precarious means, played Providence by apprenticing a destitute boy, or bought a purse of a distressed gentlewoman for £20, or otherwise indulged his "Strain of *officious Humanity*" until the consequent pleasure rose "even to Sensuality", he told his wife in the first place and the world in the second. Such actions were nobly humane and therefore proper to be exhibited. The same argument applied to his successful marriage; the record was due to society, as a proof of the capacity of human beings for "chaste and solid Transports".

After this necessary preface, we may turn to less solemn matters; for, when all is said and done, the minuet, though its strains are recurrent, does not fill a very large part of the *Genuine Letters*. More often the music quickens to a courante or a gigue, and the livelier movement was certainly more characteristic of the daily life of the Griffiths. The pleasant masculine vanity of Henry, the vivacity and petulance of

Frances, survived marriage and sufficiently vary the surface
of their correspondence. Sustained compliment was a fruit
of absence, which thus, Frances thought, improved their loves,
since in writing they took pains to express the sentiments they
were both "too sturdy to utter on a *tête à tête*". They had need
to extract honey from absence, if they could, for it played a
large part in their lives. It had been a necessary consequence
of their private marriage, in the first place, and afterwards of
Henry's failure in business—a severe apprenticeship to matrimony, during which they had learned to "elaborate a Kind of
artificial Happiness" out of the makeshift pleasures of
correspondence and "tender Regret". It is not easy to
disentangle the outward history of these years from the mostly
undated and sometimes misplaced letters, but certain figures
and incidents emerge. We see Frances at Castle-Carbury,
adapting herself a little ruefully to country life, learning to
spin, and undertaking at Henry's instance the "tremendous
Experiment" of early hours, no suppers and exercise. There
must have been something formidable to the young wife in
the instructions that reached her from her philosophical
husband. He had taken a great deal of pains, well-rewarded,
he assured her, to gain her love, and a great deal more to teach
her how to preserve his; now they must build for the future;
kindness he could promise, but the responsibility of keeping
her husband still her lover must rest with her. Under such
monitions, however, Frances plucked up heart of grace,
kindled to the moral beauty of the goal set before her, and
amused herself in her loneliness by imagining their old age
together, when companionship, surviving passion, should be
strengthened by all those accomplishments with which she
was eagerly equipping herself. One lesson she made no
pretence of learning, though it was a lesson that Henry
considered himself specially fitted to teach, for she never set
up for the least degree of fortitude. She looked upon this
virtue as the prerogative of tall, strong, philosophical men,

and as such admired it very much, but without emulation, preferring for herself the liberty of complaint. "You destroy my intire Relish for Misfortunes by your Pusillanimity", wrote Henry in tender reproach.

Presently the cradle was filled for the second time, by a little girl with a "lightning blast" on her forehead, who makes her first appearance as Kate, but soon becomes Fanchon in allusion to her mother's love-name, as her brother Richard had become Hal or Harry. Henry welcomed his children as the poor man's blessing, but he could not provide a home for them. His heaviest misfortune had fallen on him, and he and Frances were wanderers, seeing their children at rare intervals. Hal and Fanchon seem to have lived with their grandmother at Portarlington, and the boy went to school at Carlow, where his father found him "in perfect Health, Spirits and Tatters. He has only lost his Handkerchiefs and Buckles, since I left him last, but his Master says he has lost no Time." Their fresh voices ring out of the past. Harry confides his juvenile amours to his father; he has seen his sweetheart Debby's mother, judges her "*ugly enough*", and is afraid the daughter will grow like her; so he now "*has a Mind*...to be in Love with one *Kitty Hunt*, at the same school, but he will not *kiss her*, 'till he sees her Mother"—a piece of prudence that might have come from the paternal mint. He begs for a letter, and gets from a father unpractised in "*Namby-Pambicks*" an austere document, adjuring him to "act up to that Spirit and Character, which becomes your Family, and, at the same time, to behave with such Œconomy and Humility as befits your Circumstances". We do not hear what impression this address made on the sturdy little boy, who brandished a stick, like a prize-fighter, to keep his father from leaving him; his mother admired it exceedingly. Fanchon, Frances's "little mild maid", makes a more plaintive appearance as the victim of a tedious convalescence. "The poor Child longs for a Morsel of solid Food," wrote Frances, "and made me laugh, this

Morning, at her saying that, tho' Whey and Broth filled her
Belly, they *left her Teeth hungry*."

Henry notes with satisfaction the growth of his parental
sensations. They were, it seems, slow to disengage themselves
from his universal benevolence, and it was two years before
he felt a father's fondness for Harry. With Fanchon the change
was instantaneous. "She said two or three things to me which
put me so much in Mind of you, that my Heart gave a loud
Throb, and opened the Door of it to receive her in for ever."
Frances complained that she had little chance of getting to
know her children. She had had them once under her roof in
Dublin, "the third House we have been in Possession of, but
the first we could promise ourselves any perfect Enjoyment
in". Henry's library, six hundred and seventeen books, neatly
bound, had been unpacked and arranged, and Frances had
walked through every room "with great Pleasure and Satisfaction, my dear Children following at my Heels, and ad-
miring every Thing". But Dublin was not to be their abiding
place; Frances turned her eyes towards England, where she
and her husband could be more closely in touch with publishers and have means to press their fortunes; and presently
the household was broken up and the elder members went
forth to spy out the land. It proved fruitful; and first Hal and
then Fanchon was sent to join the mother. The manner of
Fanchon's departure was described by Henry as "desultory",
and with truth, for he shipped her off to Chester, unprovided
with provisions or sea-store and unaccompanied except by an
old man who saw her aboard the packet. In these circumstances,
however, the philosopher's child went "skipping all the Way,
like a *Welch Kid*, as she is", consumed with impatience to get
into the ship, since she had never seen one before, though she
had read a great deal about one, she said, in her *Télémaque*.
Her father retrieved her at Chester, and was mightily proud
of them both.

Literature had not at first appeared to the Griffiths a means

of livelihood. Frances is said to have essayed the stage in
Ireland and at Covent Garden, though the *Letters* bear no trace
of it; the details of Henry's conflict with Fortune remain
obscure. Some three years after he relinquished Maidenhall
he published the *Genuine Letters*, at the instance of Lady
Orrery (now Countess of Cork and Orrery), but for years they
were followed by nothing more substantial than occasional
verses by Frances and newspaper essays and letters by Henry.
Frances was diffident and disliked marketing her slender
talent. She did not covet fame and she dreaded criticism.
Later, encouraged by her husband and spurred by her children's
needs, she came to "shape her Quill" for profit, but she
endured authorship without exhilaration, and would break
from her taskwork to cry wistfully: "O, for a Prize in a
Lottery! that I might afford myself to be a *comfortable Fool* for
the Rest of my Life." Henry's case was different. He had
a strong bent towards literature, which was partially thwarted,
in that classical age, by his father's omission to give him a
regular education. He did what in him lay to repair this
mortifying want—a want so deeply felt that he once declared
it would palliate suicide, if anything could. Books went in
his saddle-bags on his frequent journeyings; he read in a
carriage, he said, as if going to execution; and his reading had
that reflective solidity, that constant exercise of the judgment
which belongs to an age when books are few. He was independent in his tastes, read Harrington and Sir Thomas
Browne and sent Earle's *Microcosmography* to Frances for her
lying-in. His strong and whimsical mind rejoiced in the
scope of the older writers, and it is possible to detect in his
style some echo of their deep mouths. In middle life he
discovered Chaucer and set him down in his enthusiasm as the
greatest, sweetest and most learned poet that ever wrote.
"I have a vast Reverence for old Poetry," he declared, "it is
richer than the new, though not so neat. I prefer a tarnished
Guinea to a burnished Shilling." Nevertheless, a curious and

catholic appreciation does not replace discipline, and Henry, flourishing his Latin as an impoverished gentleman may insist on his coat-armour, still felt himself in some sort an outcast from his heritage. He meditated on the compensations. If his writings were desultory, they were spontaneous and original. He had escaped that passivity of mind which is the result of too much instruction in ready-made systems, and rejoiced in all his natural energy of thought. The consciousness of his amateur status added zest to his inroads into theology and mathematics, and he delighted, as a self-taught, free-lance philosopher, to detect professionals in error. Moreover, he found in Shaftesbury a commendation of the new way of miscellaneous writing on the ground that it harmonized with the English climate and did not intimidate would-be authors. This suited Henry's case exactly, and he quoted it in the preface to his most miscellaneous book. By now he had almost indemnified himself for his deficiencies; Hobson's choice looked like a considered election, and Henry fell into the vanity of boasting of his haste, and dashed off an extemporary requiem with the silly remark: "I do everything in a hurry." Thus it came about that when the fourth Duke of Bedford, then Lord-Lieutenant of Ireland, with what Henry proudly called "voluntary Patronage" relieved the worst pressure of anxiety by appointing him to a post in the Customs at Carrick-fergus, Belfast and Larne, the work that issued from his new-found leisure was a highly informal specimen of that most unexacting of eighteenth-century literary types, the novel.

Neither of the Griffiths is an artist; they are wits and "philosophers" of modest range but genuine impulse. Frances was a sensitive critic on daily life, and there is a pleasing gusto in Henry's dissertations, compounded of a proper respect for ideas and a thorough enjoyment of his own reasoning powers. But the Muse sustained them only for short flights. Essentially literature was to them a pastime, a private adornment of life, a further channel of communica-

tion with each other, kept free from the jostle of the day's
business. Their books are full of whispered pass-words. Henry
quotes his wife's good things and often, writing anonymously,
praises her work. Frances borrows her husband's sentiments
for her male characters. Their most frequent allusion is to a
romantic dream of Frances's youth, which Henry, then
unknown to her, had shared, of a castle by the sea where
shipwrecked princesses should repay hospitality with the
recital of their lives. The oddest of the compliments, however,
is to be found in Henry's *Triumvirate*, where Carewe, anxiously
supervising the reformation of his former mistress, reads to
her Frances's dramatic poem, *Amana*. Carewe, it must be
explained, was Henry himself; for he was the most autobiographical of novelists. Not content with a single appearance
in this, his first book, he subdivided himself into three, and
performed the same feat by his wife. He is Andrews, Beville
and Carewe, "like Cerberus, three gentlemen at once". To
Andrews is allotted the unsympathetic father, the secret
marriage and the two children; to Beville the bold schemes that
miscarry; and to both the philosophical spirit. They have,
Carewe tells them, "revived the credit of ancient philosophy,
and restored to poverty its former dignity". It is pleasant to
observe one-third of Henry paying this magnificent compliment to the other two-thirds; and so he must have found it,
for he had the grace to smile. As for Carewe, in him is
perpetuated Henry's unregenerate youth; and this part of the
book was written with so lively a pen that Frances was
seriously perturbed. It must have added to her embarrassment
to see in the yielding Eloisa yet another image of herself; for
the incidents in which the three heroines are involved, where
they are fictitious, are shaped by that sort of reverie which
proceeds from a supposition. "Suppose Frances had died in
childbirth...", and there follows the moving picture of
Andrews's grief, with Hal and Fanchon, his two motherless
children. "Suppose she had been a married woman...",

and we have Beville's silent devotion to Ethelinde. "Suppose she had been less stedfast in denial...", and here Henry deplorably let himself go. The manuscript was sent off in instalments to Frances, who read herself out of breath with delight. The first volume charmed her, though she raised a little protest at being put to death so prematurely. "I own my weakness, I felt awkward about it. What would you think, if you saw me take out my Penknife and dart it through your Picture?" The second volume came in for both praise and blame, staunchly delivered. She cannot have read unmoved the passage where Carewe, hearing the cries of the woman who is bearing his child, "felt like Jaffier, when he had betrayed his Friend to the Rack"; and she found Carewe's confession of faith the most rational system of Christianity that she had ever read—an opinion shared by the author, who turned to it later to confirm himself after a course of Bolingbroke's scepticism. ("One's own arguments", as he truly said, "have generally a better effect on the Mind than those of others.") On the other hand, there were some passages that displeased her extremely, though less as a critic than as a woman and mother, who "would not have a Father write anything, which he would not chuse to have his Children read". Henry bowed gracefully to her reproof, but, though he assured his wife that the "reprehensible Blots" were put in merely to conciliate the booksellers, he refused to delete a word. He enjoyed exercising her modesty at his own expense; it was a double gratification. Five years later he walked into his next novel, *The Gordian Knot*, arm in arm with Frances. They are Mr and Mrs Sutton, the examples of perfect wedlock, the friends and guides of young lovers. The lady, we suspect, was idealized in point of fortitude and steady reasonableness, for Henry, when provoked, can hold her over his wife's head. "*Mrs Sutton* was a little ashamed of you last Post", he writes.

They cherished each other's fame with warmth, and would dash into the lists in defence of the most minute grammatical

points. Henry reports to Frances all the compliments that
she has earned by her novel, *The Delicate Distress*, telling her
how "a very pretty Miss Berkley" read it with such attention
that "she suffered her Cap to take Fire, but said that she
quenched it with her Tears", while another young devotee "sat up
all Night to finish it, as she expected to fall in Labour every
Minute, and that it would, she said, have disturbed her Mind
in Articulo Vitae aut Mortis that she had not finished it". And
then Henry refers to the book he has on hand himself, the
so-called *Koran*, an imitation of Sterne, and casually quotes
the remark of a friend, that "the Soul of *Confucius* breathed
through it", which seems to Frances a very apt description.

These letters are part of the intermittent correspondence of
the Griffiths's London years. Henry was often in Ireland, on
some sort of legal or electioneering business, leaving his wife,
as she once exclaimed in crisp irritation, "like a Citizen's
hanging Garden, to wither out of a Window in the Heat, Stink,
Smoke and Dust of London". The proportion of circumstance
in their letters is unfortunately not high, for both writers
preferred speculation and sentiment; nevertheless, enough was
recorded to serve as marginal illustration. We see Henry, on
a trip to Scarborough, bathing with a lady who fell into a
hysterical convulsion in the sea, and later, writing *The Gordian
Knot* in a garden-house, while Sterne, a recent acquaintance,
drops tears on the memoir of Henry's life. We see him on his
comfortless journeys, drenched in the saddle or shaken in a
coach, delayed from day to day at Holyhead while Frances's
letters to him rest unopened in the very post-house where
he is staying, and, finally, landing late at night from a small
boat on the "Desarts of Howath", after two days spent in
weathering an adverse wind. In all circumstances his active
mind finds something to report. The common people of Wales
have a passion for defacing the mile-stones; the coachman has
knocked all his passengers' heads together by pulling up in
mid-career to save a lame gosling, limping across the road;

a fellow-traveller has insisted on returning the barking of every village cur "till both the puppies grew hoarse with yelping". In fine weather there were the delights of the scenery, the "excessive Mountains and stupendous Rocks" of Wales, for which Henry had a strong taste, preferring them to the "richest Prospect of an improved Champain", since they enlarged the area of his mind and were associated in his imagination with the great epics of the world—the *Iliad, Odyssey, Æneid* and *Paradise Lost*.

Meanwhile Frances at home orders snuff and table-cloths from Ireland, calms her household of frightened maids when the new cook takes to seeing ghosts, and writes in her little dressing-room from eight in the morning to four, until her fingers are as much cramped as her genius. We see her moving in the literary world, meeting her fellow-novelist, Mrs Brooke, hearing Dr Johnson "with attentive veneration", and experiencing from the conversation of the blue-stocking Mrs Montagu "the placid effects of music". For leisure hours there were visits to Windsor and walks in the gardens of the British Museum with Fanchon, when that young lady had not disordered herself, as she sometimes did, by eating fruit. Her stomach was as weak and her appetite as ungovernable, said Frances, as her father's. But Frances herself was not proof against outbreaks of her old love of dissipation. "I am ill, my Harry," she writes plaintively, "and do not deserve to be pitied, for I have not gone to bed by candlelight this week past." Her health gave Henry some concern. Mrs Sutton's susceptibility, said her husband in *The Gordian Knot*, with a mixture of regret and pride, was too strong for her nerves, though not for her virtue. There had been at least one serious illness, during which Henry was shocked out of the delusion that his breast had become "the modern Porch of all ancient Philosophy"; and there were numerous smaller ailments, fever and headaches, lassitude and oppression of spirits, rheumatism, sore throats, sprained ankles and knees (which

set him asking jocosely: "What is the Reason that you are
eternally hurting One or other of my handsome Legs?") and
a recurrent weakness of the eyes, when Hal, that "comfortable
Child", read *Samson Agonistes* to her and made her laugh, and
Henry addressed her as "My dear Blinkard" and insisted on
her sending for Gataker. But in point of interest Frances's
ills must yield to Henry's remarkable colic. This was
characteristically an altogether exceptional affection. It was
variously diagnosed as due to nerves, bile, worms and "*Wind
alone*", and Henry treated it at different times with opium,
blisters, horseradish emetic, immersion in the "Hygean
Waves" of Weymouth and Scarborough, and simple starvation. It distressed him most on a journey, as once on the road
to York, when his agonies and retchings were compassionated
by the whole stage-coach company; but experience taught him
to make terms with his "unperforming Stomach". When
travelling he ate no meal but supper; three gingerbread nuts
and a pint of white wine sustained him from London to York;
and he countered the exactions of a Welsh innkeeper, who
charged him for meat and drink he never tasted, by calling in
an old beggar woman, giving her a plentiful meal and telling
the landlord that she was his stomach. He met the pain with
a determined facetiousness and sallies of paradoxical wit. It
might, he supposed, be necessary for his health, the only exercise of a sedentary man. ("Is this Philosophy or Hysterics?"
Frances enquires.) Certainly his spirits rose at the onslaught
of his old enemy; he recognized in it the grand test of his
stoicism, continually reimposed through all the years of his
manhood, and came cheerfully to the proof. His friends
crowded round his couch to be merry at his sufferings, "to
hear me confess Wit on *the Rack*, and refine my *Ore* in the
Crucible", and Frances thrilled with mingled admiration and
distress. His physical hardihood, his constant temper, found
in her the most responsive audience, and it is with awe that
she quotes a jest made "in one of your Agonies", and records

his extraordinary faculty of falling asleep in the midst of pain, reminding him how she has lain awake many a night in anxious attention and has "been often doubtful which was a *Groan*, and which was a *Snore*".

There were other calls on his philosophy, to which he adapted himself ingeniously. In Ireland, passing over the roads that he himself had made, some ten years ago, before fortune failed him, he submitted for a while to the "many grave and serious Reflections" that his situation naturally started. It was a voluntary indulgence, he told Frances, for he had "a Spring in [his] Mind that could have vaulted with Ease into more cheerful Regions, ... but the Soul loves sometimes to rest itself in Gloom, as the Eye relieves itself in Shade". At the age of twenty-two, after a night restless with emotion, Henry had dedicated himself to a philosophy of cheerfulness, and set about cherishing the random wildfires of his humour into a steady illumination of his path through life. Endurance, tolerance and an unswerving belief in providential utility formed the basis of his code; his practical discipline was a deliberate repainting of life in radiant colours, an imposture, as he once described it, which illuded the senses only to charm the soul. This was his golden bough, his passport to Elysium; in virtue of this he saw his friends as saints, his children as cherubs, and his wife "after twenty years *wear and tear*" as "*a young virgin of fifteen years*". In virtue of this he discovered a way of "*bilking* Poverty", and wrote to Frances in gay defiance: "Where my Expectation ceases, my Hope always begins." It gave him a stability and resilience of soul in which he frankly rejoiced, and a kindly sense of superiority over unphilosophical humanity, which was a good cloak against the wind and rain.

It is, indeed, chiefly Henry's character that these later letters develop. Frances alters little with time; true, her voice assumes at times a note of matronly authority, as the years approved more fully the ground of her reliance in Henry; but

she is still his "pocket Iris", still pays for her happiness by
fits of melancholy, and suffers her pen to slide into the
Melpomene strain. Her mind, she said, was the true wet-
nurse of woe. Her eyes are drawn towards the evening and
the twilight. Folding her husband's clothes during one of
their separations, she thinks at first gratefully of the many
lively, polite and kind things he said to her in them, but soon
her fancy, caught by the insignificance of "the Tenement
without the Tenant", presents to her a body after the soul is
fled, the tears gather and she becomes unfit to pursue her task.
Again and again she quotes, as if it were an emanation of her
own personality, the words of Mrs Greville's *Prayer for
Indifference*.

> Nor Ease nor Peace that Heart can know
> That, like the Needle true,
> Turns at the Touch of Joy or Woe
> But, turning, trembles too.

"Your last was in a very cowardly Stile," comments her
husband; "I am ashamed of you." In him we have a nature
broader-based, cherishing his own idiosyncrasy, watching with
profound interest his own evolution and duly grateful to his
Maker that he is able to approve it. He marks with pleasure
his own growing orthodoxy, deletes the Arianism from the
second edition of the *Genuine Letters*, supplements the simple
dictates of reason with revelation, and begins to talk of a
"*lively, saving Faith*". If the arguments by which he established his new position were still highly individual, he had at
least the satisfaction of feeling himself coming into line. He
accepted human nature, and the verdict of the reasonable
majority of it, without misgivings though not without
scrutiny. The frailties of men did not affect him tragically,
and he cheerfully compounded for their errors and for his own.
His sense of humour was strong and pervasive, but scorn set
no edge on it; though it went beneath the skin, it never went
to the marrow, and when he laughed at himself he never

shrank under his own laughter. It is with a painless sense of
the interesting oddities of the mind that he recounts to
Frances the "most lucky Accident" by which he first became
aware that he loved her. He was shaving one day and, to wipe
his razor, took up one of the letters of "Chloe", Frances's
predecessor in his affections.

I am apt to make Reflections upon all Manner of Occurrences;
and recollecting that Time was when I would sooner have sacrificed
a Bank Note, or worn such a Beard as Signor Dolorida's in Don
Quixotte, I immediately began to perceive that my Passion had
been extinct...a considerable Time before; but how long I could
not exactly determine, because I could not precisely compute how
long I had been in love with another Object, whom in the very
Article of Shaving, I found that I had conceived a real Passion for
some Time before.

Self-knowledge and self-satisfaction are here happily balanced
in the scales of humour; but a man cannot always defend
himself against ridicule, even by laughing first, and there are
pages in the *Genuine Letters*—the author's anxious defence of
his literary independence after a few days in company with
Sterne, for instance, or his disinterested concern about a pretty
young hoyden "at the dangerous Crisis of Fifteen"—which
must raise the sort of smile that Henry would not have
expected.

He had the straight-faced mirth of his countrymen, a delight
in saying the oddest things with a sincere countenance, and
found, like Goldsmith, that in England his wit was not always
seconded by the forward child, understanding. He had a
natural love of paradox, which set his lively wits to work, and
he retained through life the delight in fluent and cheerful
nonsense that had caused his brothers, in boyhood, to christen
him Mr Nimble Gob. It is Mr Nimble Gob who debates
with his wife which of them, in right of ancient Welsh blood,
has most claim to a Kingdom in North Wales, and proposes
that she shall submit to "the Test of the *true Prince*, by going

with me to the Tower, and referring the Decision to the Lions there". It is Mr Nimble Gob who describes a painted ceiling as a *"fricassy* of Cherubims, with here a Head and there a Leg or an Arm, peeping through the Clouds, which look like a good, rich, thick Sauce, poured about them", or records his interview with the modest apothecary and man-midwife of Holyhead, who prescribed worm-powders for his "Disorder" and showed him, in a phial, "a Worm of the most extraordinary Structure I ever saw...something like a Garden-slug ...[with] a Hood on it, which resembles a Shagreen Case", recently removed from a lady patient "after a tedious Process". Lastly, it is Mr Nimble Gob who, disgusted at the strained pathos of the contemporary novel, proposes to unite the plots of *Clarissa* and *Sidney Biddulph* and conclude with the execution of the two heroines at Algiers, "finger by finger, toe by toe".

Young Harry inherited his father's energy of mind as well as his musical tastes. The references to him become more frequent as he advances towards manhood and his future becomes a matter of concern to his parents. Banking and the army were considered, and for the latter, at least, Harry must have had some taste, since he left his Academy in London to flaunt away at reviews in Hyde Park and at Bagshot, and had to be summoned to Windsor and pinned to his mother's apron-strings. At last, through the offices of a friend, he was appointed cadet in the East India Company's Service, and in his sixteenth year put away childish things and settled down with all his father's method to prepare himself for his station in life. We hear no more of Ranelagh or reviews, for the boy applied himself to his studies with such remarkable perseverance that he allowed himself but four hours' sleep, and his mother in alarm sent him to Signor Angelo for fencing lessons, an "Exercise absolutely necessary to his Health". "Tell my dear Boy", wrote his father from Ireland, "that I received his English, French and Latin letters, and am extremely pleased with them every one; but am in too great a Hurry at present to answer so universal a Scholar." Frances bought him books and music as part of his equipment for India, "and by the Catalogue he has shewn me, he means to carry over a perfect Library, if you will indulge him". All in all, he was "just such a Boy as childless Kings would kidnap", and his parents called him the Nabob, and pinned their hopes to him. Indeed, Fortune was more auspicious to this Richard Griffith than to his father; he did become a Nabob, returned to Ireland before he was thirty, bought the estate of Millicent, Kildare, and played a notable part in Irish politics and agriculture. Millicent sheltered the last years of Henry and Frances, and there Frances saw the grandchildren on whom her imagination had so often dwelt. One, a boy of eight when she died, inherited in full measure the intellectual force and scope of his family, and put it to fruitful use; he became Sir Richard John Griffith, the civil engineer and the first great figure in Irish geology. But these events are still far in the future when the *Genuine Letters* close with the stir of Hal's departure and with a characteristic spurt of temper from the overwrought Frances, while Henry in the midnight stage from Chester, troubled with rheumatism, colic and a severe fit of the gravel, but full of a pleasant mixture of self-approbation and paternal and conjugal affection, travels night and day to give his adventurous son his blessing.

"I hate your replying to peevish Paragraphs of mine," wrote Frances, on receipt of one of her husband's rational point-to-point missives; "God knows I have forgot them myself before they reach *Lombard Street*." A philosopher, however, does not easily relinquish a chance of displaying his philosophy in action, and Frances had often to see her darts fall blunted from that broad shield, to be forgiven, teased, embraced, and thereafter shown with tender reproach the drop of blood which one malicious point had drawn. This treatment never failed; and certainly, although it falls short of perfect charity, it is neither unwise nor ungenerous. It did not break Frances's spirit, which moved with equal spontaneity to waywardness and submission. She had the gift of quarrelling with grace and in accepted security; her railing was but broken music and her harshest letter a *"most elegant Scold"*. As for Henry, he found a relish in these mimic revolts. A love of power and authority is natural to men, as Frances pointed out in her addresses to young married women, and in such encounters Henry felt his power pleasantly and therefore used it sparingly. Moreover, "there may be few things more grateful to a generous mind, than to have *something to forgive*". They exercised their various emotions briskly; and then came *amoris integratio*, the full close: "Let us break each other's Hearts no more." Even in remonstrance they preserved that politeness which they both regarded as essential to the married state. It was a word much on their lips. "Good Breeding", wrote Frances, "is absolutely necessary to keep the most delicate Affections alive." Constancy is not enough, there must be gallantry as well, or the marriage will fall into that state of bluntness and satiety which the Griffiths triumphantly avoided. This was their grand discovery, their contribution to the theory and practice of wedlock—the polite marriage. On this ground they built their happiness. Early in their life together Henry had concluded a dissertation on matrimony with an application of St Paul's words, *Let those who are married live as those who are not*, which would have surprised their author. Surely, he remarked, a wife was an object worthy of *les petits soins* as well as of the greater duties? The standard of deportment should be kept up. A careless and slovenly air strikes chill into the fond sensations, and then, "how unspirited, how indelicate an Obligation is Duty sole!" For himself, he preserved carefully as a husband the polite attentions of courtship, and occasionally drew his wife's attention to the fact. Presents were dispatched to Hyde Street, when he set out on his travels, accompanied by cards gallant enough, Frances said, to hurt her character; to which the donor replied agreeably: "The Tenderness and Politeness of our Loves have absolutely refined Matrimony into Amour between us." In return, he got letters so kind and flattering that an old friend, to whom he showed one, told him that he must have either a very strong head or a very stupid one, to trudge about the streets like a person of no note or consequence, while he was receiving such apotheoses every post. But Henry's head was strong enough to stand a good deal of this kind of thing from his "dear Panegyrist". They kept anniversaries scrupulously and often poetically. Henry inscribes four quatrains to Frances *Anno matrimonii XVIII*, and she recalls in verse that it is now a score of killing winters since she first dedicated a poem to him, while their letters are sown with reminders that it is this day three months since they parted, or fourteen years since their wedding day, or twenty-one since first they loved. Ten years after her marriage, Frances, shuddering in a chilly bathing booth at Dunleary, had pencilled on its wooden wall a prayer to sea-born Venus to renew her youth and keep her lovely in her husband's eyes; but, as they grew older, both of them took a pleasure in the contrast between their homely appearance and the romantic ardour of their affection. She was, she said, a little, quiet, inactive mortal and he a plain, clumsy man; but they were the guardians of a transfiguring flame.

Homely indeed Elizabeth Griffith looks in the picture of her by Pyne that hangs at Hendersyde Hall, Kelso, whither her great-grandson, Sir George Richard Waldie-Griffith, must have taken it, when he transferred his home to his mother's estates in Roxburghshire. This is not the young Frances who sat in Ireland to Hussey for a pencil drawing, but a middle-aged woman, whose charm is gone. She has light brown hair and a long nose, and her features have the slightly swollen aspect that suggests prolonged ill-health; she is wrapped in a white shawl and holds a quill pen. As one looks at the picture one recalls her headaches, her bad eyes, her querulousness, the plaintive, graceful, flattering, deprecating letters that the pen indited to Garrick—appeals for work, suggestions of adaptations from the French for his theatre, pleas for help and criticism, apologies for having lost her memorandum of his advice, and unhappy reproaches at his delays; and then one sees, lying on a book at her left hand, a paper inscribed *To Frances*. The companion picture, also by Pyne, is described as Richard Griffith of Maidenhall, and shows a young man[1] with dark hair, wearing a brown coat open at the neck and directing his gaze upwards to the right for inspiration; suitable adjuncts in the shape of paper, a book and a large quill pen lie to hand. This is perhaps the picture of which Frances speaks in her letter on *The Triumvirate*; that which hung in their London house seems to have displayed Henry in another attitude, since Frances, describing her return from a supper-party, full of gossip, to a contemplative husband, says that he sits looking at her in silence, like his own picture on the wall above, "with mild Complacency and philosophic Acquiescence".

They accepted the homespun, but insisted on the golden thread that ran through it. It is useless to try to disentangle it; it was part of the chosen fabric and pattern of their lives. "Adieu my only Object," writes Henry at the end of a letter; "thank God I have Delight in you." She was his "very best Child in the World", his "sole Possession in Life and chief Hope in Immortality". She quickened him. Her presence gave him full possession of his senses; her absence rendered him a very Stoic. Even in Heaven, he told her, he would yield only a philosophic Approbation to the Dispositions of Providence until she approached to bring his Sensations home to him. And, trembling, she prayed to die first.

[1] If Pyne stands for Robert Edge Pine, the portrait painter, it is difficult to account for Henry's youthful appearance. Pine was born in 1730 and Henry must have been nearly forty, at the least, before he could have painted him.

There is a postscript to the story of Henry and Frances that will please cynics. It is found in the letters of the fastidious and elegant Miss Seward. She had met the Griffiths at Lichfield in 1776, and had failed to acquire feelings of friendship for a woman who gave no evidence of much power of mind, or for an ugly fellow, who wore a wig, was covered in snuff and apparently past middle life. However, she corresponded with Henry for some time in a tone of gay familiarity; he called her Frances the second, and she smiled loftily at his groundless vanity; she thought she distinctly perceived in him a libertine imagination. In 1793, when both the Griffiths were dead, a correspondent brought up their names, and the Swan of Lichfield expressed her disdain at some length, finishing with a tit-bit of scandal.

Griffith and his wife did not live together during several years prior to his death. Have you forgotten an event of which the public prints of the day were so full? His seduction of a girl of fortune and consequence in his grand climacteric, and her elopement with him? I have always understood that he lived with that fair unfortunate the remainder of his days. Thus ended the boasted attachment of Henry and Frances, whose published letters were so much admired.

Miss Seward is unreliable, but it would be rash to ignore her story. I have not yet traced the elopement in the public prints. Dates are a difficulty, even if we do not press too closely Miss Seward's "grand climacteric". In 1782 Frances, publishing her *Essays addressed to Young Married Women*, spoke of thirty years of happy married life. In 1786 the six volumes of the *Genuine Letters* were re-issued with a new subscription list, in which many old friends and patrons appeared and to which many respectable names were added. It seems unlikely that either of the Griffiths would have taken this step immediately after a domestic collapse. In February 1788 Henry died in his son's house at Millicent. Some scandal there must have been, which rumour attached to the name of Richard Griffith, though obituaries, which sank that name in the better-known Henry, ignored it. Truth has not come to light; but if Miss Seward's paragraph is in any way allied to it, and if anything of the old man remained in Henry after the passing of so stormy a climacteric, it must have grieved him to have broken his record so near the close, and he must have perceived with disappointment—however accustomed to compound for human nature—that it was only Carewe who lay on the death-bed at Millicent. Andrews and Beville, like Beauty and Discretion in *Everyman*, had abandoned him at an earlier stage of his journey.

THE DIDACTIC LYRE

∧∧∧∧∧∧∧∧∧∧∧∧

PEGASUS between the plough-shafts, Apollo's hands tarred over with the surgery of Admetus's ewes, are rare sights nowadays, but they have not been rare in most ages of literature. A few poets have taught and many pedagogues have poetized, and a form of verse which began in primitive charms and mnemonics came to be cultivated by scholars for the sake of the problems it set and for the triumph of their own cool ingenuity. To impose elegance upon recalcitrant material was perhaps in most cases the prevailing intention of the poet when he strung and tuned his didactic lyre; but his professed aim should not be too lightly dismissed. His subject was sometimes near his heart, and in that case he co-operated in the spread of enlightenment and might indulge a reasonable hope that his poem, especially when finely bound and embellished with engravings, would penetrate to quarters beyond the reach of a prose equivalent. Such were the hopes of Dr Hugh Downman of Exeter when he sent to the press the successive instalments of his poem *Infancy*, breathing the wish that even in hostile America mothers might be the better for his advice.

Downman was born in 1740, the son of Hugh Downman of Newton House, Newton St Cyres, Exeter. He passed from Exeter Grammar School to Balliol College, Oxford, and in 1763 was ordained in Exeter Cathedral. But his advance in life was not to lie through the Church, and within a year or

two we find him at Edinburgh attending the medical school
and boarding at the house of the blind poet and orator,
Dr Blacklock. The immediate cause of the change seems to
have been Miss Frances Andrew, daughter of Dr John Andrew
of Exeter, the Thespia of Downman's elegies and the
"Unwearied Guardian! Tutoress! Lover! Friend!" of his life.
For Thespia he became first a poet and afterwards a physician.
His stiff, embarrassed proposal is recorded in an early poem
with the veracious energy which was his usual speech on
Parnassus—a speech that is never less than manly and not
infrequently rises to eloquence, though it seldom comes
within a wing-beat of poetry. In his pastoral invitation to
Thespia, nevertheless, there is a snatch of clear tunefulness and
April colouring for which no other name will do.

> Oh come my Fair One! I have thatch'd above
> And whiten'd all around my little cot,
> Shorn are the hedges leading to the grove,
> Nor is the seat and willow bower forgot.

Miss Andrew, however, was well-connected—her mother was
the daughter of Sir William Courtenay, Bart., and sister of
the first Viscount Courtenay—and the cot and willow bower
were felt by her relations to be an insufficient provision for her;
the lovers had to submit to separation, and Downman went
off northward to study medicine, as a first step to an assured
competence, launching behind him Parthian shots of versified
invective at the "avarice" of his elders.

He found that exile had its pleasant side. He made lasting
friendships with his host and with the other young medical
students in the house, and saw himself favourably placed for
the growth of his stripling Muse. Dr Blacklock's own poems,
as we read them in the double columns of Chalmers, do not
provide us with many inspiring pages, but undoubtedly there
must have been inspiration in a household where medicine,
theology, music and poetry were continually practised and

discussed, where the master carried a flageolet in his pocket and the mistress, no poet herself, once celebrated her husband's birthday in couplets, as a mark of her veneration for his poetical character. Her ingenuous lines called forth some pretty verses from Downman. Melissa, he writes, straying idly round Parnassus, gathered one rose-bud, for which, since she had no passport, Calliope chid her; but Hymen, recognizing in the wanderer "our Blacklock's wife", interceded on her behalf and she was allowed to carry home her spoil.

Downman's lyrics, however, in spite of occasional felicities, are pale beside the amazing temerity of his didactic verse, and to this we must turn, brushing aside odes, elegies and the imitation of Spenser which, read aloud, beguiled Dr Blacklock into liking that poet at last. It was after he was married and settled in practice in Exeter that Downman projected and began to execute the poem by which, as contemporary critics did not omit to say, he testified his two-fold allegiance to Phoebus Apollo, the Healer and Singer. The first three books of *Infancy, a Poem* were published successively in 1774, 1775 and 1776. The price was low. A shilling put each section of this "humane and sensible poem", as the *Monthly Review* called it, at the disposal of the young bride and bridegroom to whom the author so urgently recommended it. Next year the three books were published together for two shillings, but it was not until 1788 that Downman completed his original design and issued the fourth edition in six books for half-a-crown. He had been delayed and discouraged by ill-health, the result of the years of sedentary study and reckless overstrain in his youth, and in 1788 he had been forced to retire from practice; but Thespia had led him back to his versing, and on the shore at Dawlish, where he went for the bathing, and among the apple groves and willows on the banks of the Alphin near Exeter, he had wooed at once Hygeia and the Muse. Happy Thespia, whose part it was to solace a talent by an orderly and modest hearth, and not to contend in baffled love, as more hardly proved women have done, with the unappeased forces of genius, scattering the brands. To Downman, zealously inverting the garden mould with his new-found strength, the experiences of the years of illness shaped themselves into the fable of the nymph Gymnasia, whom Minerva presents, after the opening of Pandora's box, as the only saviour of the wretched human race. He had known the misery of a strong and benevolent man who feels the egoism of an invalid blunting his mind and weakening his "nobler passions". He had watched wretchedly the waning of "that instantaneous sympathising glow", in which his generation saw at once the greatest moral luxury and the special mark of civilized man; and he was painfully convinced of the connection between our "thinking substance" and the "vile mould" of matter. "Virtue and vice on exercise depend", he cried with abrupt boldness in the fifth book of *Infancy*, and consigned cradles and go-carts to museums. But this line of thought was too disquieting, and, having delivered his warning, he shrank from the abyss and raised his eyes to where the "cherub Hope join'd hand in hand with Faith" soared through the heaven of the eighteenth century.

There are plenty of celestial figures in *Infancy*, for Downman, who could write simply when he wrote for Thespia, entered on this serious task in a complete panoply of poetic diction, and conciliated his readers with personifications, inversions, circumlocutions, apostrophes and every handsome adjunct of a didactic poem in Miltonic blank verse. Tinsel decorations he expressly disdained, but he did very assiduously scatter before the steps of Truth and Science the not infrequent flower. Flowers, he felt, were necessary, if his poems were really to advance his "darling wish of public good", but he had no mistrust of his subject, and perceived no radical incongruity between the accent of poetry and:

> Angina, apthous Sores, Eruptions dire,
> Pertussis fierce, and squalid Atrophy.

After all, he stood in an accepted tradition. He could invoke
a number of "pure ethereal Bards" who had nobly stooped to
instruct mankind—Akenside, Mason, Beattie and, especially,
Armstrong, author of *The Art of Preserving Health* and like
Downman a physician—and it was in confident pride that he
joined the hallowed band of those who

> round the flowing locks
> Of Fancy cast the sacred wreath, enwove
> By the fair fingers of Utility.

It was no mere verbiage. To him the fingers of Utility were
fair, even when employed on less pleasing tasks than weaving
wreaths. He expected to have some difficulties with the
details of his subject. Armstrong himself, the "Parent of the
Prophylactic Lay", had approached his section on Diet with
misgiving, and the reader, following his daring step "through
paths the Muses never trod before", stumbles on such
obstacles as

> Tertian, corrosive scurvy, or moist catarrh,

before he reaches the final grandiose vision of universal decay,
and hears the grave voice intone:

> The Babylonian spires are sunk;...
> Achaia, Rome and Egypt moulder down...
> This huge rotundity we tread grows old....

Nothing daunted, Downman launched into his subject.
His lights are reason and nature; his grand foe is ancient
superstition, too often incarnated in the figure of the midwife.
On the threshold of the poem she stands, a sinister figure,
preparing for the newborn child the poisonous drench that
custom sanctified and advancing science condemned. The
child, however, instructed by nature, is wiser in its wants and
demands, "plain as expressive signs can ask", the mother's

breast; and here Downman backs up his plea for maternal
nursing by one of his best explanatory passages.

> Know, the first Efflux of each milky Fount
> Is Nature's chymic Mixture, which the Attempts
> Of bungling Art cannot supply; this flows
> Gently detersive, purifying, bland;
> This each internal Obstacle removes
> And sets in motion the young Springs of Life.

The physiology of the nursing mother inspired him with
some of his most intricate evolutions. For he has not done
with the subject. If the mother cannot or will not nurse her
child, there is the wet nurse to be selected. The choice must
fall on a peasant, a robust countrywoman, one whose cot knows
the step of cleanliness, "Attractive Nymph"—and how painless a sublimation is this of hard scrubbing! She must be
neither too young nor too old,

> For torpid or impair'd by frequent Use,
> The flexile Vessels, which convolv'd in Maze
> Wrapp'd within Maze, secrete the purer Stream,
> Their Office will more sparingly perform,
> Or less nutritious Particles supply.

But to insist on exact correspondence between the nurse and
mother in age, colouring and temperament is to be idly
scrupulous.

> Excess thou should'st indeed avoid
> Of Plump or Lean, nor would I choose th'adust
> And highly bilious, or the sable Hue
> Of clouded Melancholy.

Here the foster-mother is dismissed, but the cardinal theme
of nutrition is pursued through two more books. Never,
perhaps, had the youthful stomach received its full dignity
in verse before, though Downman's eloquent discussions of
rickets, regular meals and a fruit diet do not reach quite the
lurid force with which his predecessor, Armstrong, had described the inception and progress of a bilious attack in the

adult organs. That passage must be sought in its original context; it is too disturbing to transcribe here.

The third book ends with one of those digressions which the didactic poet was bound to cultivate. He turns from "th'intestinal Maze", from wine ("Destructive Bacchus"), water ("the blameless Fluid") and preserves "acid, or salt, or saccharine" ("Pickles, salted meats, and sweetmeats," says the Argument more explicitly) to reprove the advance of luxury and apostrophize the primitive virtue of Britain. Pegasus, docile beast, makes for the open country with lumbering gait. A few pages since, his rider had been negotiating a reference in verse to porridge—

> milk in various forms
> With rice, or other farinaceous grain
> Inspissated...;

now he heads northward, his mind rekindling with the memories of his student years, to the land where the contagious air of luxury has not yet penetrated, whose sons and daughters, "perfect in their Kind", still cherish a pristine virtue, where in his youth he sat at the feet of Gregory or helped to crowd the lectures of Cullen. It is pleasant to see his verse starred with the names of his old masters—Monro, Hewson, Hunter, Black—and pleasant to find him defending the hardy young men, the modest and merry girls of Scotland against the "rancorous lie" of Southern pride. So should hospitality be repaid.

Half his task yet remained to be performed. He had to persuade "Elegance, coy Nymph" to accompany him while he discussed clothing and temperature—"unanimating themes" —and gave a cursory glance at children's ailments. The last section was fairly manageable, especially now that he had modified his original plan of recording in detail the symptoms and treatment of the principal diseases to which the infant is liable—a "green design", in his present judgment, fit only to

scare mothers or to make them conceited; but over clothing
the nymph was more restive. She barely allowed the in-
structive bard to recommend light garments, to cast a pathetic
retrospect at swaddling-bands and to express some mistrust
of pins. After all, there was no need to elaborate.

> Bright glows the warm maternal soul
> And clear, illumined by a hint alone.

But over cleanliness he was more emphatic; the mother must
supervise her nursemaids with meticulous care, lest the babe—
and here Elegance, repenting, addresses herself magnificently
to her task—

> by the corrosive sting
> Of acrimony pierced, tormented shrieks.

Counsels of hardihood follow, cold baths, constant exercise,
a hard bed; the British physician, like many of his generation,
turns approving eyes upon the young Brazilian and Canadian
savage, and the accustomed names of Tiber and Eurotas sound
in his verse; but he is wisely moderate and proposes no extreme
measures to the polished daughters of his age.

As he nears the conclusion of his poem a certain rigour of
utterance takes the place of his usual grave urbanity. Once
more upon the page rises the intolerable figure of the
"vaunting midwife", presuming upon her nostrums and
barring the door on "th'ingenious Leach", while, within, the
"little lively cherub", drenched and poisoned with her drugs,
slips out of life. It is with no ignoble professional pride that
he entreats the mother not to trust the "babbling hag", not to
delay summoning the physician, and holds before her the
melancholy story of Evadne, whose child perished of its
grandmother's amateur doctoring, and who heard, day and
night, the inward reproach: "Thy child is slain, and thou wert
an accomplice." Let her think on this, and avoid betimes the
immedicable sting of remorse, the only evil that the human

soul cannot master. But Paean's votary must not end on such a note, and he bids the mother turn to more joyful prospects,

> to where thy child
> Hath, by inoculation, overcome
> The plague Variolous,

and to that great benefactress, Lady Mary Wortley Montagu, who suffered the experiment to take place on her own son, for which act of resolution and patriotism he would have statues raised to her throughout Europe and America. With a last strain in her honour, crowded with nymphs and swains, nimble feet and polished foreheads, flowery garlands, fauns, dryads, youth, health, wisdom, humanity, and all the other half-personified objects of his poetical and medical attention, Downman lays down his genuine lyre.

He had made a vigorous bid for the combined fame of a poet and a philanthropist, and there are lines which suggest that he found the measure of his reward disappointing. His critics were consistently favourable, but, as one of them pointed out, the mothers and nurses capable of profiting by instruction so classically conveyed cannot have been numerous. He recognized that he was writing for the few. During his lifetime they were enough to send the poem into nine editions, but their number has not increased. An artist, as Keats observed, must serve Mammon; he who serves the God as well, and survives in spite of his divided allegiance and the change of fashion in his divinity and its cult, must have Titanic thews indeed.

Infancy was Downman's last sustained poetical performance. His health was re-established, and after some years' intermission he was able to ~esume practice in Exeter. Poetry was renounced, except for the yearly elegy to Thespia on her wedding day, and that took on, as time passed, a homelier and more humorous style. The work that he published after 1784 —his *Tragedies* and new and enlarged editions of his poems—

had been composed chiefly during his retirement. Turning the pages of these old volumes, with their corroborative supplement of friendly eulogy by Devonshire gentlemen and grateful patients, the reader finds himself full in the track of the early romantic movement. There is the deliberate suffusion of colour, the search for nervous and forcible expression, that manifest in many an obscure versifying corner at this time a discontent with Augustan urbanity, a desire for more exciting poetic experiences. "Emphatic" is one of Downman's favourite words; in his *Ode on the Death of Harold* he bids the minstrel "pour for him th'emphatic verse", and for Thespia he even sheds an emphatic tear. He read and admired the Elizabethan dramatists, and endeavoured to imitate their spacious eloquence in his plays. The best of these, *Lucius Junius Brutus, or the Expulsion of the Tarquins*, was never performed, and, though Downman apprehends the passion and horror of his story and expresses it to a degree beyond what contemporary usage permitted, it cannot honestly be contended that the stage lost very much. *Belisarius* and *Editha*, which reached the stage in Exeter, made greater concessions to dramatic convention. Downman had hankered for Shakespeare's freedom to bring on Belisarius, the fallen general, as a beggar, but had felt obliged to deny himself an audacity which his age, solicitous for tragic dignity, would have found indecent. *Editha*, an amalgam of the usual dramatic emotions of the eighteenth century, is remarkable for nothing except its local theme, the siege of Exeter by the Danes. The Danes, indeed, were very well combed by the time they appeared on the Exeter stage, but, free from this constraint, Downman preferred them in their natural wild condition. Like Gray, whose influence is apparent in his poems, he sought to renew his imagination at barbaric founts. He followed well-pleased the steps of the Muse as she roved through savage nations, and tasted the "beloved, deceptive rills" of fancy where they spring from the well of fiction, high among the Gothic hills.

Gray's *Descent of Odin* suggested the verse into which he translated from the Latin *The Death Song of Ragnar Lodbrach*. It is a ringing metre enough, but the abruptness of the orignal has to suffer expansion to fill the mould. *Pugnavimus ensibus* cries the poet, and in Downman's version this war shout becomes:

> With our swords' resistless might
> We have thinned the ranks of fight,

while *Non est lugenda mors* appears, even less tolerably, as

> Unmoved I quit the realms of light.

It is odd to find this benevolent eighteenth-century gentleman nourishing his poetic inspiration on the battle-sweat and the raven's banquet; but it is not unprecedented. He felt in the *Death Song* "a species of savage greatness, a fierce and wild kind of sublimity, and a noble contempt for danger and death", which gave some reflection, however distorted, of his own combative manhood. In groping for a poetry that should once more express the whole man, he and his contemporaries were bound to overstress those deep instincts which the last four generations had left unsung. In effect, they submitted to a metaphorical blood baptism and rioted in ideal slaughter. Downman renders and heightens the carnage in every verse. By the end of the poem he is total gules.

But these orgies were the rare indulgence of a sedate and magnanimous nature, of a physician who was esteemed for his sagacity and widely beloved for the blameless simplicity of his manners. In Exeter he and Thespia grew old together. They were not rich. During his illness, Downman speaks of living "close or the verge of want", and pens a vigorous address *To Independence* in which he refuses to pay an obsequious attendance on "the many-acred blockhead"—not, one hopes, one of his wife's noble relations, the Courtenays. Their resources must have increased when he resumed practice; at least, he could afford to take time for the pastimes in which he delighted.

In 1792 he founded a society of twelve members who met to dine, talk and read papers to each other. Some of these papers were preserved and published in *Essays by a Society of Gentlemen at Exeter* (1796), and it is worth lingering to glance at Downman's literary circle, for it is characteristic of the little groups of readers and modest practitioners of poetry up and down England who were discussing at that time the failure of invention in poetry and the need of new poetical subject-matter. It was planned, as the writer of Downman's obituary in the *Gentleman's Magazine* records, "to unite talents of different descriptions and genius directed to different pursuits", and it occasionally gave its attention to scientific enquiries, but its main topics were literary and historical. The Reverend Richard Polwhele, antiquarian and satirist, Downman's friend and patient, was a member, and so probably were some of the amiable poetasters whose work he publishes in his *Poems, chiefly by the Gentlemen of Devon and Cornwall* (1792). But the bright particular star was the Reverend Richard Hole whose *Arthur; or, the Northern Enchantment. A Poetical Romance, in Seven Books,* had received on its publication in 1789 what seems to us such inordinate praise. This poem, which is like a large wardrobe of romantic apparel, designed to adorn the gestures of passion but displayed upon stands which reproduce the didactic and domestic groupings of the eighteenth century, seemed to many critics to signify the dawn of a new era in poetry. The author was modest but spirited about it. His romance was an attempt to share the pleasure that he himself had felt in Gothic fictions. It claimed kinship with Ariosto. True, he was not prepared to admit a complete severance between epic and romance, for the incidents and manners of the romance, like those of Homer, were frequently drawn from nature. "The delineation, however, of these manners, has been but a secondary consideration. This performance is chiefly referred to the tribunal of Fancy, and if there condemned, it makes no further appeal."

The pleasure that Hole took in his ramblings in mythology
and legend is obvious all through his poem. He can hardly
bear to leave anything out. He begins with a storm in the
Hebrides, raised by the three Weird Sisters, who are a mixture
of the Northern Parcae and the witches of Macbeth; lets
Arthur take service with the Byzantine Emperor and fight
against the Crescent; provides him with Hengest as a rival for
the hand of Merlin's daughter, Imogen; introduces Odin and
Stonehenge, and Laplanders fighting for a Norwegian lord
against the battered Britons, and fills up the chinks with
Ossianic Irishmen, spectres, demons and fairies. The couplets,
which have a certain careful picturesqueness, are full of literary
reminiscences, while notes refer the reader to Malet's *Northern
Antiquities*, Hurd's *Letters on Chivalry and Romance* and
Whitaker's *History of Manchester*; and when Hole has boiled
everything together and taken off the scum, the residuum is
a very heavy poem indeed. The best moments for the modern
reader arise unintentionally from the search for the forcible
which, since it sprang not from a vigorous imagination but
from an intellectual perception of the tameness of contemporary poetry, often resulted in a mixture of the violent in
sentiment and the prim in cadence. Such a passage is the
death of Hengest, of which Hole writes unperturbedly:

> Deep in his breast he feels the deadly wound,
> And gnaws in bootless rage the unconscious ground.

Pack his poem as he might, Hole had to leave some of his
hobbies unrepresented, and to these he refers in his preface.
He was interested in mythology and legendary lore, especially
in the links and repetitions of theme between the myths of
different nations. He believed, for instance, that the author
of the *Arabian Nights* must have known Homer. He looked
for a clue to such relationships in language, and here he had
a playfellow in Downman. Among the published essays of
the society there are notes on the origin and mythology of

serpent worship and on the worship of sun and fire, which the writer of the memoir in the *Gentleman's Magazine* ascribes to Downman. They are signed T.V. in the book, which suggests a literal Latin translation of the writer's surname. The biographer regards his subject's flighty passage through Judea, Egypt and Greece with some misgiving and remarks that "pursuing the track of Mr. Bryant, he chiefly rests on the insecure and delusive basis of etymology". Jacob Bryant's high-handed marshalling of supposed cognates in his *Analysis of Ancient Mythology* did stimulate the Exeter gentlemen to grope curiously among the roots of language, and if the results were rather amusements of the fancy than contributions to knowledge, this was not out of harmony with their aim. The study of comparative mythology might be expected to produce raw material for poets, but it had so far no serious effects on the minds of the students, and Hole in his cool eighteenth-century way describes his investigations as "a blameless though not a very important pursuit".

They addressed poetry as "Enthusiastic Maid" and hoped to nourish her enthusiasm on material that was blameless though not very important. Here is a fatal discrepancy between means and intention. Nevertheless, if we shift our gaze beyond this generation, we see that their activity had results more important than the *Northern Enchantment*. Their classical and romantic sports presumed a certain training, and, like Spenserian parody, required attention to the real thing. Hole left in manuscript a translation of the first Eclogue of Virgil into the Exmoor dialect. Such an undertaking may be partly jocose, but it must unseal a wellspring of vigorous speech to run with illicit, refreshing music in the jaded poet's ear. Polwhele, amusing himself and the society with an ironical defence of the characters of Shylock and Iago, was taking up, behind the barricade of mockery, an attitude towards the persons in Shakespeare not very unlike that of the romantic critics, for he was regarding them as historical figures, capable of existing in some other relation to the reader than that in which they are placed in the plays. Downman supported his *Vindication of the Character of Pindar* by translations of two of the odes which, though they clip the ample pinions of the Theban eagle to the roots of the feathers, do testify by their mere existence to a thirst for grandeur which is not made void of significance because it does not yet seriously incommode him. In time of drought these prudent gentlemen dug channels which the Spring rains were to fill with impetuous beauty.

In 1805 Downman retired from practice, and about this time the literary society was discontinued. A second collection of essays is said to have been prepared for publication, but it never reached the printer. Downman lived just outside Exeter at Alphington, where the Courtenays owned the manor; and here in 1809 he died.

His countenance and Thespia's in middle-age were recorded by his distant kinsman, John Downman, and Hugh Downman's portrait, a "stained" drawing, was reproduced for the frontispiece of the 1809 edition of his poems. It is a regular face, with an open forehead under the wig, a strong, well-proportioned nose and chin, and a firm mouth with a full underlip. The eyes light the face, dark, full, wide-open, and further emphasized by strong, dark brows. One receives an impression of masculine resolution and judicious benignity. Thespia is his complement. No more in her youth, she has lost what claims to beauty girlhood may have given her, but she has preserved a certain piquancy of feature, a feminine pliability and charm of expression, that are still attractive. The old friends and housemates have worn well. The critic who reviewed Downman's last publication, *Poems sacred to Love and Beauty* (1809), and looked anxiously among the new poems to see that no fresh object of affection had supplanted Thespia, was soon reassured; Downman was staunch. Page after sensible page testifies in the confident tread of its quatrains to the durability of an affection which had outlived the "grateful tumult" of youthful ardour, but still warmed the hearth by which Downman sat reading, Thespia by his side and a cup of wine at his elbow. The strength of his verse, like the pleasure that it can at times evoke, is not strictly poetical. Candour, energy, a solid intellectual content, a dignified but unpretentious style, these are his qualities. His elegies are considered statements of experience—"good, substantial, thick-wove stuff", he called them in later years; they miss achievement by a certain slowness of pulse, and the best are those of his youth in which the beat is quickened by momentary jealousy and controlled desire. The control, the scrupulous regulation of his emotion, which Thespia's confidence claimed from him, was perhaps less favourable to his poetry than to his domestic happiness.

> My breast is not with vulgar passion fraught,

declared the lover.

> I glory in my dignity of thought,

and though Thespia touched him to fine issues, they were seldom poetical.

Almost, one could dismiss his volumes as near-poetry, gratifying to human nature but negligible as art; almost, but not quite. A nerve thrilled in him. He has directness of attack—a resonant simplicity in the opening line of a poem, that recalls Sidney. He has a sudden tender phrase for the Devon landscape, for Alphin's scanty stream, for the wood of tufted elms, the orchards, the hills of Ide and the "small, but verdant fields", and it is against this green background that he sees Hygeia in the dawn,

> Piercing through some covert yet untried,
> Beating the moist, o'erhanging boughs aside...
> The sprinkled dewdrops glittering in her face.

He has a sustained vigour of mood and expression that sometimes flashes into passion, as in the *Madness of Aspasia*, where

he captures something of the wild fancy of the seventeenth-
century mad-songs, or the bursting cry with which, at the end
of a painful misunderstanding with Thespia, he longs to hold
her and gaze on her "till the nerves of vision fail". Critics
wished that he would polish his lines more, but for that he
had apparently no inclination. He spoke his mind fairly in
verse and left it at that, and the reader never doubts that these
were indeed his very feelings, even when the metrical mould
is plainly imitative. This authentic note rings through the
borrowed cadence of the little ode on independence.

> How lives the man, whose thoughts have broke
> Imperious Custom's servile yoke?
> Him Nature, guiding by the hand,
> Leads on where Truth and Reason stand;
> Virtue her mantle round him flings,
> And Honour waves her silver wings.
> He dares not stoop to foreign laws,
> But wisely courts his own applause.
> Health beams delighted from his eye,
> And Innocence walks smiling by.
>
> When sinking in the vale of years
> His head the hoary foliage bears,
> Backward he casts his tranquil sight
> And views each scene reflected bright;
> No sullen damps his joy infest,
> No plagues of Avarice tear his breast;
> Him willing Duty hastes to serve,
> And strains with zeal each labouring nerve,
> While Love stands gazing on his face,
> Intent the latent wish to trace.

He knew the foothills of Parnassus, though he never climbed
the peaks. He won no prize, but in the race of poetry, "not
without dust and heat", he also ran.

THE BRISTOL MILKWOMAN

⋀⋀⋀⋀⋀⋀⋀⋀⋀⋀

THE name of Ann Yearsley, the Bristol milkwoman, is to be found in histories of Bristol, in the literary reviews and magazines between 1785 and 1796, and in the private letters of some amateurs and patrons of letters at that time. It is also to be found on the title-pages of a novel, a tragedy and three collections of rather ungainly verse. She was one of the uneducated poets of the eighteenth century, and had her share in the welcome accorded by a literary public, apprehensive of the failure of genuine poetic fire in a regulated world, to any writer who could exemplify the primitive force of genius. That she composed spontaneously when, as her patroness, Miss Hannah More, assured the public, "she had never even *seen* a Dictionary", that misery and want, though it had changed her voice to a groan, had been unable to silence it, somehow renewed the faith of her readers in the validity of poetry. If, under one aspect, she was a painful and meritorious scholar, with all her century's belief in Education, Social Love and Enlightened Humanity, under another she was more august. She was the savage priestess, rapt by the god whose attentions to her civilized contemporaries were apt not to exceed polite calls. She could rank with the Lapland and Chilian singers who bear witness, in Gray's ode, to the omnipresence of the Muse. She was a living proof to the supercilious critic, as Miss More exultantly declared, "that genius is antecedent to rules and independent on criticism".

When, therefore, Miss More and her friend, Mrs Montagu, undertook to sponsor Ann Yearsley's *Poems on Several Occasions*, they had no difficulty in marshalling an impressive body of subscribers. The nucleus was that society of "blues" of which Mrs Montagu was Queen, together with their accustomed male allies, such as Dr Burney, Horace Walpole and Sir Joshua Reynolds, but the subscription list penetrated many circles, and was carried into the Church by Miss More and into the aristocracy by Mrs Montagu, so that peers and bishops stood ranged under every letter of the alphabet to encourage the milkwoman in her ascent of Parnassus. It was a brief splendour. Within a few weeks of the publication it was known that Mrs Yearsley was not turning out well; she had quarrelled with her patroness; prosperity had made her arrogant, and nature, it appeared, had made her malicious, since she was devising and spreading impossible slanders about Miss More. The large and respectable body of subscribers experienced a shock of disappointment and a reaction of cynicism, and the milkwoman's prospects were irretrievably hurt. Some friends stood by her and she gained others, enough to make a noisy party in Bristol, where her story appealed to those who did not like Hannah More; but the tide of her fortune had ebbed, and the anxieties and disappointments of her last twenty years seemed to Southey, when he surveyed them for his essay on the *Lives and Works of Uneducated Poets*, to compose a melancholy story. He saw it as a story of frustration, however, not of empty pretension, for in her work he discerned the proof of extraordinary talents and an ardent mind, continually thwarted in utterance. "She was no mocking-bird," he concludes, and his justification lies in her published writings; for here, with clumsy symbols and in the abstract terms that fashion dictated, she has written the autobiography of her heart and mind. There is little of the circumstantial detail that one would like to have, though something can be retrieved to supplement Hannah More's account of her and the scraps of information available elsewhere, but her emotional experiences, her metaphysical questionings and moral conclusions, the scars and trophies of her painful conflict with life, are here legibly, though awkwardly, inscribed.

Ann Cromartie, daughter of John and Ann Cromartie, was born on Clifton Hill, on the outskirts of Bristol, and baptized on 15 July 1752 in Clifton Parish Church. Her mother was a dairywoman—a milkwoman as it was then called—and brought her daughter up to her own business. The milkwomen of Bristol were a well-known class, with traditional customs and a traditional dress of their own. They poured into the city in the early morning from the Somersetshire and Gloucestershire villages round, balancing their milk pails on their low-crowned, broad-brimmed beaver hats, and crying: "Hae any muilk?" as they went. On May day they planted a maypole on the downs, and the innkeepers of the neighbourhood, according to ancient custom, lent them their silver plate for the celebrations. One of the portraits of Ann Yearsley shows her in this milkwoman's dress, with a cloak and kerchief, and the big flat hat worn over a cap. Mrs Cromartie's care did not end when she had provided her daughter with the means of livelihood; she also taught her how to live. The industry, the exact probity, which Hannah More admired in her milkwoman had been fostered by the strict counsels of the mother. Together they walked in Clifton Churchyard, and Mrs Cromartie drew her text from the emblems of mortality carved on the tombstones and strove to accustom her daughter's mind to the thought of death; but the girl, though her imagination did not reject the grand subject, brooded on it in her own way, and it was already the way of poetry. "I marked the verse," she wrote later; "the skulls her eye invite." Words and metre pleased her, and the occasions of pleasure were not confined to the rhymed epitaphs on tombstones and mural tablets, for her mother, who delighted in books, borrowed from "her betters" such volumes as they would lend. Now, or in her early married life, but most likely before domestic cares crowded her days, Ann read Young's *Night Thoughts, Paradise Lost*, Pope's *Eloisa*, some Shakespeare and a translation of the *Georgics*, which appealed to her specially. Her reading was necessarily fragmentary— when Hannah More met her she had never heard the names of Dryden, Spenser, Thomson or Prior—but it was sustaining and productive, and she fed her imagination further by studying the "little ordinary prints" of classical subjects which hung in a shop window. She was taught to write, a more unusual accomplishment for her class than reading, by her dearly loved brother, William.

Behind this thin outline of a laborious and eager youth we can stretch, with assurance that she was not blind to it, a prospect of Bristol and the countryside. Clifton Church still lay among meadows and footpaths, a quarter of a mile outside the city boundaries, but from the hill one could look down on the docks, watch the passage of shipping along the Avon and hear at times the clamour of returning seamen. These shouts echo in lines of hers, full of pride in her native town's commerce:

> Joy tunes the cry; the rocks rebound the roar,
> The deep vibration quivers 'long the shore;
> The merchant hears, and hails the peeping mast,
> The wave-drench'd sailor scorns all perils past;
> Now love and joy the noisy crew invite,
> And clumsy music crowns the rough delight.

Eastward sparse lines of handsome freestone houses were reaching round Brandon Hill to join Bristol to Clifton, while during her lifetime Clifton itself and the little spa of Hot Wells, down by the Avon, expanded into streets and crescents. But the eye passed easily over these gratifying signs of prosperity, southwards to the hill of Dundry, westwards across the Avon gorge to Leigh Woods or northwards to Clifton Down, topped by its windmill. These sights, with the lower reaches of the Avon and the distant mountains of Wales, were familiar and dear to Ann; she had listened to the stirring of the wild creatures in the woods, and gone out at dawn to tend her beasts in the upland fields, and the wide view had filled her with a vague elation which she transferred to the young countryman in her poem *Clifton Hill*, as he strides in Spring through the open air:

> The landscape rushes on his untaught mind,
> Strong raptures rise, but raptures undefined.

The undefined raptures of the untaught swain presently focus themselves on the opposite sex, and the writer, conscious of a staid girlhood, has her word of regret for random loves. She herself was married on 8 June 1774 to John Yearsley, an honest and sober man, says Hannah More, but of a turn of mind very different from her own; a correspondent to the *Gentleman's Magazine* ten years later described him as "of no vice but little capacity". The marriage was witnessed by her brother, William Cromartie, and by Elizabeth Morris, and took place in Clifton Church. Round this church her life moved in narrow compass. Clifton Hill became both her Delectable Mountain and her Hill of Difficulty, and somewhere among the landmarks whose names she affectionately repeats, unknown to all eyes but hers, lay the graveyard where Despair's blind victims stumble, and the byway to Hell.

It is still ten years before we get the first direct sight of Ann Yearsley. In the interval she bore six children, of whom the eldest, a boy, died, and lost her brother, after whom she named her second son, William Cromartie Yearsley. He was perhaps a seaman. She said goodbye to him on the banks of the Avon, already a tragic stream for her, troubled with the death, by accident and design, of three of her friends. Of these sorrows and many others she was afterwards to make verse, often clumsy but never feeble, and bearing in each strenuous paragraph the print of experience. But in these years of motherhood, poverty and hard work her poetical impulse was rather a torment to her than a joy, since the act of creation remained imperfect. Composition was for her an intense activity; she tried later to describe its process, the sudden rising in the mind of the strong image, the "substance-seeking Shade", craving embodiment and "resolved to shoot into the World of Things". But at this time she was tongue-tied, and could give no form to her struggling notions.

> Oft as I trod my native wilds alone,
> Strong gusts of thought would rise, but rise to die;
> The portals of the swelling soul ne'er op'd
> By liberal converse, rude ideas strove
> Awhile for vent, but found it not, and died.
> Thus rust the Mind's best powers.

She craved for education and for communion with minds like her own, and, as these were beyond her reach, poetry festered in her. Yet something was written down, for it was by her poems that Ann Yearsley first became known to Hannah More. This was in September 1784; but the Yearsleys had passed the highest point of their distress some months before. A working-man's family, including five small children and an old grandmother—for Mrs Cromartie shared their home— must live, however thriftily, on the edge of want, and the severe winter of 1783-4 brought them to extremities. Ann Yearsley was expecting her sixth child, and her plight and that of the whole household which, remarks Hannah More, "I am afraid she had too carefully concealed", was discovered only at the eleventh hour by a Mr Vaughan—probably Richard Vaughan, Esq., of St Michael's Hill—who found them almost dead of starvation. The landlord had taken the cows; the famished husband sat by the hearth of his stripped cottage; old Mrs Cromartie lay bedridden in a corner on a heap of straw, and the children were crying for food. He saved the parents and children, but the grandmother was beyond his help, though she lived to see it arrive, and on 23 March she was buried in Clifton Churchyard. It was a woman crushed and listless under this heavy grief that Miss More went about to assist.

Hannah More was at this time just under forty, a successful and respected woman. She lived in Park Street, Bristol with her four sisters, but spent much of the spring and summer in London with Mrs Garrick and in visiting the country seats of her friends. She had won brilliant successes on the stage and in literary society. The elderly bluestocking ladies had petted and made much of their recruit; Garrick had super-intended the production of her tragedy *Percy*, and Dr Johnson had teased and flattered her, and listened with emotion to the account of the five More sisters, devoted to each other and to their work of educating the young. Since Garrick's death, however, she had begun gradually to withdraw from society and had already forsaken the theatre, for her *Sacred Dramas* admitted no connection with the green room. She stood midway in her life, looking back not without complacence on her worldly triumphs, and forward with grave intentness to years of retirement and arduous Christian enterprise. In Bristol, her native town, she was very much of a personality, a lively, cultivated woman, demure and a wit; warmly affectionate to her sisters and friends, but balancing her sensibility with practical good sense. She had many admirable virtues, and knew them for what they were. She had rectitude, benevolence, enough moral courage to keep a strict Sabbath in the circle of Garrick and Horace Walpole, and enough human weakness to take pleasure in the reputation it earned her. Her reason taught her that humility was essential to the spiritual life, and her will imposed it upon a nature not in the first place apt to be humble. She was sincerely pious, and her piety, deepening with the years and no longer satisfied with Sundays and the casual devotions of a fashionable life, began to claim all her time. She had set her feet on the path that led to the retreats at Cowslip Green and Barley Wood, and to the establishment in the face of obloquy of the Cheddar schools.

The prospect was not yet clear, however, nor had the labourer learnt the sedate and uncomplaining charity, the chastened acquiescence under attack, which were so notable in her later years. She was, perhaps, little accustomed to failure and disappointment. When, therefore, on her return from Sandleford, Mrs Montagu's country house in Berkshire, she was shown by her cook a copy of Ann Yearsley's verses, it was without any misgivings that she undertook to arrange the poetical milkwoman's affairs.

She went to work prudently, but with real goodwill. She had been struck while reading the verses by "a certain natural and strong expression of misery, which seemed to fill the heart and mind of the author", and, after careful preliminary enquiries into her character and history, she went to see her in her cottage on Clifton Hill. She had expected, perhaps, and would certainly have rebuked, some pretensions in the "poor enthusiast"; she found a perfect simplicity of manners. She gave her a guinea from Mrs Montagu as an earnest of patronage, and presently arranged to make her a small allowance during the preparation of a volume of poems to be published by subscription. It was not without hesitation that she resolved on this course. She was convinced of the genuine spirit of poetry in the verses, but she dreaded lest publication should unsettle the sobriety of Ann Yearsley's mind, and, "by exciting her vanity, indispose her for the laborious employment of her humble condition". For her condition, though it might be raised above misery, was and must remain humble; she must not be seduced into devoting her time to the "idleness of poetry", nor transplanted out of her natural surroundings; she might perhaps exchange the work of a milkwoman for that of a village school-dame—such a project, then or later, was on foot among her friends—but it would be wrong to encourage her to look above her station. Mrs Yearsley's character, however, reassured her, for she was industrious and appeared to an uncommon degree convinced that the making of verses was not the great business of human life. Miss More's own motives upon examination also appeared pure. She did not feel herself actuated by the idle vanity of a *discoverer* in bringing to light genius buried in obscurity; she wished primarily to secure the bread of a meritorious woman. Moreover, Mrs Yearsley's talents were certainly in themselves the gift of God, and: "It would be cruel to imagine", concludes Miss More, "that we cannot mend her fortune without impairing her virtue." There is no need to question the general honesty of Miss More's account of her scruples; but she was perhaps less indifferent than she supposed to the opportunity of enlarging her own consequence, and of combining her old and new characters in a last gracious appearance in the literary world as the discreet mentor, the bountiful sustainer of plebeian genius.

What Hannah More meant to Ann Yearsley can be seen on page after page of *Poems on Several Occasions*. She did not yield readily to the influence. She was sunk in apathy, in a solitude and darkness of soul more tolerable than the pangs of complete consciousness, and she tried to reject her guest's arousing ministrations. Looking back, she calls herself surly, stubborn, unnatural, "more savage than the nightly-prowling wolf". She had seen riches abused, and regarded the well-to-do with hard suspicion; and though Miss More extorted her admiration, it was mixed with "sullen envy". Here indeed was despair and a soul brought near to denying its Maker, and the sight stimulated all that was deepest in Hannah More. Her words—the sacred words of promise and reproof—broke up the long frost, and the "corrected soul" of her penitent turned to her in a glowing fervour of gratitude. This fervour alone prevented the association from being painful to Ann Yearsley, for she felt keenly the contrast between this cultured woman and herself, "uncouth, uncivilized and rudely rough". Hannah More had had access from childhood to the knowledge which poverty had put beyond the milkwoman's reach. She had learnt Greek and Roman history, sitting on her father's knee, while he recited to her the speeches of her favourite heroes, first in the original language to gratify her ear, and afterwards in English. Only a radiant humility could contemplate this gulf without bitterness, and such humility, though for a while it dominated Ann Yearsley, could not be the final station of her mind. Already there are discords. Stella—it is her poetical name for Miss More as Lactilla is for herself—has accused the author, with much reason, of flattery "and of ascribing to the Creature that praise that is only due to the Creator"; and the answer comes with a sudden change of tone that is almost a snarl:

> Excuse me, Stella, sunk in humble state
> With more than needful awe I view the great.

Gratitude is already almost an oppression to her; her pride, that savage and anti-Christian virtue that Miss More sought so steadily to subdue, wins once more to speech and finds a bitter flavour on the tongue. A benefactor—she calls him Theron—has cancelled his charity by what she considers a betrayal of confidence, and she cries out against the vanity which, in the disguise of friendship, will explore the treasures of a heart and "basely heave Her hoard of woes to an unpitying world". True friendship, that "noblest ardor of the soul", is so rare that only ethereal spirits can enjoy it; what is generally offered as such is a bright delusion. She herself has never owned a friend; and though, as she writes the sullen phrase, she sees Benevolence and Pity start back in hurt surprise, she maintains her point. She cannot give to the "instantaneous act of bounty bland"

> That name which never yet could dare exist
> But in equality.

On this bold note she breaks off. Some months later the shrewd Miss Seward, reading this passage aloud, paused, as she tells us, to ejaculate: "Ah Yearsley! thou hast a proud and

jealous spirit, of the Johnsonian cast. It will be difficult to
oblige thee without cancelling the obligation by the manner
of conferring it."

During the winter and spring of 1784–5 both women were
busy preparing for the publication of Ann Yearsley's book.
Miss More copied the manuscripts and revised them to the
extent of providing punctuation, eliminating grammatical
errors, and possibly suggesting some changes of diction, but
she made no attempt to polish into elegance the wild vigour
of the rustic muse. The poems, though sceptical readers
doubted it, were not only substantially but literally the milkwoman's. But her work on the poems was but a small part
of Miss More's activity. Subscriptions were to be raised and
the literary world informed of the project, and here she proved
herself an industrious and adroit agent. Horace Walpole was
approached with specimens of Mrs Yearsley's poetry and the
news that she had read his own *Castle of Otranto* with enthusiasm; the great ladies in Bath and the neighbourhood were
interested, and the milkwoman was sent for to Stoke to visit
the Duchesses of Beaufort and Rutland, and to Bath to Lady
Spencer and Mrs Montagu; Fanny Burney, paying one of her
last visits to old Dr Johnson, talked to him about Mrs Yearsley,
and the venerable Mrs Delany herself circulated the proposals.
Other friends helped to raise and sustain curiosity about her.
In December an account of her appeared in the *Gentleman's
Magazine* in a letter from an unnamed gentleman living on
Clifton Hill. He has met her, and praises her modesty and
dignity. She is plain, he says, but not disagreeable to look at
and has a good singing voice. We have some record of her
appearance. An engraved portrait by Lowry, probably
idealized, was published in 1787, showing her in her milkwoman's dress, with her hair knotted simply under the large-
brimmed, low-crowned hat. In the same year a far more
interesting portrait by her friend, Miss Sarah Shiells of
Lambeth, was exhibited in the Royal Academy and engraved

in mezzotint by J. Grozer. It shows a sturdy woman, seated at a table, writing. She wears a short-sleeved gown, an apron, a folded kerchief with a black neck ribbon, and a big mob cap, under which the hair is dressed in curls. She leans on her left elbow, raising the forefinger of the left hand conventionally to her cheek; the right holds a pen and is tracing on the paper before her the first lines of her self-explanatory poem, *To Mr V---n*. She has no pretensions to beauty, but her strongly marked features, arched brows and steady, challenging eyes are, as her contemporaries would have said, "informed with Mind". Joseph Cottle, who knew her well, said that she evinced even in her countenance the unequivocal marks of genius.

Poems on Several Occasions came out in June 1785 and was well received, though then as now what interested was not so much the poetry as the figure of the melancholy and ardent nature struggling to surmount a barrier of ignorance of which it was painfully aware. This was, wrote Miss More's friend Weller Pepys sympathetically, a new intellectual phenomenon. "She seems to have a conscious dignity of mind", admitted Horace Walpole, "which I like better than her verses, and which is a greater rarity than middling poets or even than middling poetesses." Dignity is the word that always occurs in descriptions of Ann Yearsley and her work; but the dignity of a middling poetess, deficient in liveliness, could not please Walpole for long, and in a few weeks, wearied perhaps by a subject that "Saint Hannah" thrust on him too persistently, he is giving it as his advice that, when poor Mrs Yearsley shall have been set at ease by the subscription, she should drive her cows from the foot of Parnassus and hum no more ditties. It was two or three months before the professional critics expressed their opinions, and then they were kindly enough, though they gave no support to Mrs Montagu's surmise—if indeed her hyperbole is meant to be taken at all seriously—that the humble milkwoman, instructed only by the study of

Milton and the Bible, might rise above Pindar and step beyond Æschylus. Pindar and Æschylus were not in question; as they saw, her master was Young in his *Night Thoughts*; but they were able to find qualities they could honestly approve in poetry that had cost so much in the writing. They were the same qualities that Hannah More and Walpole had agreed in observing. Mrs Yearsley had a naturally good ear for blank verse, and a spontaneous wild imagination abounding in simile and personification. She was, in short, something better than a mere curiosity, but how deep the roots of poetry ran in her they were not prepared to say on the evidence of one book alone. But long before the reviewers had given their verdict to the world, the quarrel between Miss More and her protégée had become common property, and a great deal of kindly patronage had been permanently lost.

The main grounds of this quarrel are clear, the details disputable. Mrs Yearsley published her account of it in a *Narrative*, dated 12 October 1786 and prefixed to the fourth edition of her *Poems on Several Occasions*. Miss More made no public statement, and her story must be pieced together from her correspondence and the accounts of her biographers, composed fifty years after the event. The occasion of trouble was a deed of trust, sent down to Ann Yearsley for signature on the publication of her book, by which she and her husband renounced all claim on the profits, which were to be invested in the names of Miss More and Mrs Montagu and expended by them, when and as they thought fit, for the benefit of the milkwoman and her children. Miss More's intentions were of the best; she could trust her own discretion but not that, perhaps, of Mrs Yearsley nor certainly that of her husband; and she did not foresee that what seemed to her a necessary safeguard must strike the vehement, proud woman as an insult. "I felt as a mother deemed unworthy the tuition or care of her family," she writes in her *Narrative*. Her patroness was away from Bristol at the time and had asked for an immediate return of the deed. The eldest Miss More, to whom Ann Yearsley carried it for advice, remarked—probably as a strong argument to induce her to take this unpleasing step in her own interest—that if her sister chose to say she had but twopence of Mrs Yearsley's, she might, "for the *world* could not get it out of her hands". But the thought of dependence and submission, which seems to have had an abstract beauty for the Mores, was less assuaging to the milkwoman. The deed was signed, with a reluctant hand and a despairing mind, bent chiefly on avoiding the charge of ingratitude which is so intolerable to the peasant's mind. John Yearsley, labourer, added his signature.

This was on 10 June, and by the end of July the breach between Hannah More and her "poor Enthusiast" was complete. On her return to Bristol, Miss More had invited the Yearsleys to her house to explain to them the disposal of the profits, and the meeting had ended in an outbreak of stifled resentment on Ann Yearsley's part. The scene of the disagreement comes out vividly in the milkwoman's sarcastic, indignant *Narrative*. She had scrupulously handed over to Miss More every guinea of subscription money she had received, and had exceeded the allowance Miss More made her during the preparation of the book, so that she was now in debt to the extent of £10. Miss More gave her the sum, out of what she regarded as her own earnings, with ungracious admonitions; and when she came to prefer her eminently reasonable request for a copy of the deed of trust, there must have been some desperate bluntness in her manner to make her patroness exclaim, as we hear she did: "Are you *mad*, Mrs Yearsley? or have you drank a glass too much? Who are your advisers? I am certain you have drank, or you would not talk to me in this manner." Miss Betty More intervened; there was a return to kindness on Hannah's part, and Ann Yearsley withdrew in emotion. But the trouble was not to be patched up. Mrs Yearsley's proposal that she should be admitted as joint trustee, that she and her husband should forgo all claim on the principal but should receive the interest without control, and that the money should be divided according to the number of her children and subject to their demand on reaching the age of twenty-one, seemed to Hannah More impossible to accept. There were subsidiary causes of friction. The Duchess of Devonshire had given Mrs Yearsley Bell's edition of the poets, and Miss More had kept them for her till she could provide herself with shelves; now she wrote to the Duchess, complaining that the books were withheld from her. Miss More ceased to see her protégée, and when they met after three weeks for a final interview, it was formally, in the presence of witnesses. In the interval, to Miss More's annoyance, the stubborn peasant woman continued to fetch the dishwashings from the Mores' kitchen to feed her pig; she had paid the cook for them, and they were her right.

According to Mrs Yearsley's *Narrative*, Miss More met her with an imperious austerity of tone. She rebuked her as a savage and bad woman, then went through the accounts and offered her the first half-year's dividend on the money invested in the funds, "which, with so much insult," Ann Yearsley writes, "I could not accept; but told her calmly, that she had rendered obligation insupportable already, and I never would make it more oppressive". Both women claim to have been calm, but their notions of calmness may have differed. Miss More's friends said that Mrs Yearsley threw the money—ten guineas—at her head, and that she, with controlled meekness, terminated the scene with the prayer: "May we never meet till we meet in Heaven." Mrs Yearsley declared that the money lay untouched on the table. She got her copy of the deed and asked for the manuscripts of her poems, both those selected for publication and those omitted; they were, of course, important to her; in a few weeks Horace Walpole was to set it about that Miss More had "washed and combed the trumpery verses", and there would be need of evidence to confirm friends and stop the mouths of detractors. But there would be no evidence.

Miss More replied, "They are left at the printer's, Mrs Yearsley. Don't think I shall make any use of them—they are burnt." "Burnt!" said I!! She seemed confused—my heart felt for her.

As Hannah More had offended the mother in Ann Yearsley, so now she offended the proud energies of the conscious though imperfect poet; she had regarded the verse simply as marketable ware, to be exchanged for warmth, food, a measure of security, and had allowed what was unmarketable to be destroyed. Twice her confident benevolence had blinded her, and she found the results of her bounty painfully disappointing. There was indeed £350 in the funds, still under her control, but in place of the gratitude and mild content she had hoped to plant, she had run her hand into a thorny crop of disillusion and recrimination. She withdrew with reticent dignity.

These events were a nine days' wonder in London, but in Bristol they were the source of a prolonged feud. Bristol, proud of its literary standing, would have liked to cherish both its poetesses, but found this difficult enough in the circumstances. The feat, however, was achieved by Joseph Cottle in his *Early Recollections*. He knew them both personally, calls them "in genius, compeers", and gives, involved in verbiage, a very reasonable account of the quarrel. The mistake lay, he thinks, in Ann Yearsley's pleading her own cause and in her impetuous manner. What did an ignorant milkwoman know of stocks? She saw in the money a means of educating her sons and opening a circulating library, and a judicious friend could have explained this to Miss More. Delicately, he hints a fault in the benefactress.

Both parties meant well, but from the constitution of the human mind, it was hardly possible for one who had greatly obliged another (and the recipient in a subordinate station) to experience the least opposition, in an arrangement, deemed by the principal, expedient, without experiencing, at least an uncomfortable feeling....[There must have existed] a predisposition to misconstrue motives, as well as a susceptibility, in the closest alliance with offence....Here was a strong-minded, illiterate woman on one side, impressed with a conviction of the justice of her cause; and further stimulated by a deep consciousness of the importance of success to herself and her family; and on the other side, a refined mind, delicately alive to the least approximation of indecorum, and not unreasonably, requiring deference and conciliation.

This essay deals with Ann Yearsley, to whom this disaster was cardinal and indelible, not with Hannah More, who survived it easily in reputation and less easily, perhaps, in spirit, and came to see it, no doubt, foreshortened very far in the distance, as she passed her extreme and honoured old age on Clifton Hill. Yet, for the completeness of the story, which is that of a clash between two notable women, we must turn aside to see her, in the months following the quarrel, in a light a little different from that shed on her by her admirers.

Surprised and disappointed, she would willingly have kept the miscarriage of her charity secret; but this the angry milkwoman would not allow. People visited Ann Yearsley and asked to hear her story, and she told it them as it appeared to her after weeks of brooding. It was reported that she accused Miss More of fraud and intended misappropriation of the subscription money. Such a suspicion may well have sprung up in her mind, and the building of Miss More's house at Cowslip Green at this time would seem to give substance to the charge. The notion was ridiculous, but in a violent revulsion of feeling, compounded of anger, disappointment, baffled admiration and the sudden return of a mind, persuaded into new habits of thought, to its old channels, nothing is too ridiculous to be supposed. Miss More bore herself under these attacks with dignity and generosity. She knew exactly how she ought to behave, and conformed to her own high standard; and this achievement should not be undervalued for it implies a high degree of self-conquest. She wrote to Cadell the printer to hasten the delivery of the second edition of the poems, hoping to make up the sum of the profits to £500; she continued to look for settled work for John Yearsley, and she refused, in the interests of Ann Yearsley's children, to resign the administration of the trust. She justified herself to herself in every way, and determined to do all possible good in return for evil. Her actions indeed do stand forth clear, but the ingratitude of her protégée had touched some unregenerate crudeness in her own mind; she had caught the infection of passions from which she had thought herself immune; and in the brevity of the accounts she sent to enquiring friends, and in their carefully compounded tone, part humorous, part humble, we may detect signs of dismay, which become unmistakable in her momentary spasms of disgust. It was an "odious tale", she cried when Horace Walpole applied for information; but doubtless it was a great opportunity for spiritual growth. "Had she turned out well, I should have had my *reward*; as it is I have my *trial*"; and later, when *Poems on Various Subjects* was published, she called on Walpole—an unlikely companion for spiritual exercises—to join her in "sincere compassion, without one atom of resentment" for the depraved woman. To the Reverend Richard Polwhele she wrote, struggling for balance: "You will be sorry to hear that the Milkwoman, for whom I raised £500, has turned out the wickedest and most ungrateful of the human species; but I have the comfort of knowing that her wants, which were very pressing, are relieved." As she contemplated the painful episode, the lessons she expected to learn from it emerged like a brand. "Poor human nature, I could weep over thee. Nothing but the sanctifying influence of religion can subdue and keep in tolerable order that pride which is the concomitant of great talents with a bad education."

She was not left undisturbed to re-establish her composure. Her position was untenable, and before Christmas she saw herself obliged to relinquish the trust, which passed at first to a gentleman in Bristol and finally to Ann Yearsley herself. Then, when this point was conceded, she was approached by James Shiells, Esq., of Lambeth, surveyor. This gentleman, the father of the portraitist, had arrived at Hot Wells at the end of August 1785 and had taken up Ann Yearsley's cause; he now wrote from Lambeth pointing out a paragraph, headed *Patroness and Client*, which had appeared in the *Bristol Gazette and Public Advertiser* of 8 and 10 September, in which Mrs Yearsley was accused of ingratitude, and entreated Miss More to restore the milkwoman's character and, by means of another paragraph, to put the whole matter "on a pleasant footing" once more. To this plea, however, she remained inexorable.

This was the last skirmish. In time her efforts brought her peace, and the uneasy, protesting tone dies out of her letters. Five years later she hears of the milkwoman's illness and asks her sister Martha to find out if she would take "a famous medicine", if it should be procured for her. A friend is to enquire, without naming her, for "I suppose the poor creature would be afraid to take anything of my recommending". These are the accents of charity that suffereth long and is kind. For Hannah More the struggle was now over, and she had drawn spiritual fruit and practical counsel from it. She had learnt that her nature could not bear controversy. "To see others angry", she wrote over twenty years later, "has such a tendency to make me angry, that I am afraid of getting my temper soured, and my heart hardened." Henceforth, in a life exposed to the attacks of ignorance, that threatened her great work of the Cheddar schools, she practised tranquillity and patience. As for the practical counsel, it is not, I think, fantastic to trace the reverberations of her experience with Ann Yearsley in a letter on her schools, written to the Bishop of Bath and Wells, in whose diocese they were. "My plan of instruction is extremely simple and limited," she explained. "They learn on weekdays such coarse works as may fit them for servants. I allow of no writing for the poor."

But for Ann Yearsley, undisciplined by breeding and sore with the sense of unmerited reprobation, recovery was far more difficult. Total recovery she never achieved; she never forgave or attempted to understand Hannah More. The vague sense, perceptible in her *Narrative*, that her patroness hung in some "deplorable extremity" and was also a prey to conflicting passions, disappeared; in indignant misery she etched on her mind the figure of the rigid prude, the vain and sanctimonious cheat, contemplated it for years with fixed malice, and took her revenge as she could. The experience was never wholly assimilated; she never, while she wrote, wholly cleansed her imagination of its infection; it was always capable of generating fresh poison. Not a book of hers that has not its fling against her former benefactress, and the flings are often enough ill-mannered, the jeers of an angry peasant. She acknowledges measureless obligations to Miss More in a sarcastic footnote; she learns the old story of her abortive engagement, some twenty years before, and triumphs over the "slighted prude", whose cold precepts were based on no wisdom of the heart; and it must have been in conscious rivalry that she published her poem on *The Inhumanity of the Slave-Trade* within a few months of Miss More's *Slavery*. In the throes of disappointment she reacted violently away from the doctrine and discipline of Hannah More. We have a glimpse of her in the correspondence of Miss More and Mrs Montagu, decking herself in "very find Gauze bonnets, long lappets, gold pins, etc.", and talking of putting Miss More in the papers and petitioning the King against her. No doubt she talked wildly and ignorantly, and salved her hurt pride with an arrogant defiance. She had resented being exposed as an object of charity in the introduction to her own poems, and now she began to suspect that jealousy had guided Miss More's pen when she corrected them. She summoned up her energies to prepare a new volume, which should vindicate her reputation as an independent poet, and in what she now wrote there is no induced humility. The milkwoman has got up from her knees and stands before us dilated with wrath, meeting the civilized mockery of her opponents with gestures, extravagant enough and often ridiculous, but impressive in their passion and amplitude. The censorious, she cries, may as well seek to turn the flaming sun from his direction or dash the stars with earth's pebbles as "scan the feelings of Lactilla's soul". There is too much lightning and thunder here, but it was genuine electricity.

She spewed prudence out of her mouth, and laid her whole being open to the assaults of a sensibility that Miss More had held it essential to repress. At all costs she will feel, and "Nature feels most poignant undefended". Magnanimous suffering seemed to her, then as always, the highest reach of the human spirit, the proof of the sublimest powers of the soul. It is the substance of most of her poetry, of which the themes are grief, deprivation, death, endurance, the rapture of immortality and—since in this respect the unlettered are at no disadvantage—the valour of untaught minds. It is only in the wounded bosom that virtue can exist, she declares; there it first exacerbates all sensation, "then pants with painful victory". She seems in all these passages to imply that a complete acceptance of and surrender to emotion is the first step in mastering it; that mastery is indeed absorption not rejection, and that to minimize our anguish, to prescribe the degree to which it is to be allowed to affect us, is to thwart the growth of the soul. This is nowhere explicitly stated, but it is most clearly intimated in the allusive attacks on Miss More, with whose figure she identifies all the cool discretion and regulated sentiment that seemed to her valueless beside passion. Suffering alone gives the power to minister to the grief of others more than the "dregs of vulgar consolation"; her patroness claimed to have received this seal, but Ann Yearsley questions the "vaunted grief" of those who "can fix a rule for sentiment".

As she rejected Miss More's moral guidance, so she dissociated herself even in literature from her restraint. She could not share her culture; she was consigned to ignorance, explicitly discouraged from acquainting herself with the indispensable "ancients"; but she was still a poet, though a permanently incomplete one, and she resolved to hang no clogs on her inspiration. In this mood she advises M . . . , an Unlettered Poet, in a poem on *Genius Unimproved*, to make up his deficiency in science and the classics with "artless Rapture", and to ignore all rules and precedents, consoling him with the assurance that ecstasy is strongest in untaught minds; while, in the advertisement of her new book in *Felix Farley's Bristol Journal* for 25 November 1786, subscribers are invited on the grounds that, as the volume is "the produce of her own uncultivated genius, without any alterations or corrections, she hopes [it] will prove an amusing novelty to those who prefer Nature's unclipt wing of poetic fancy". This brief document, with its aggressive allusions to "the mean artifice, and false representations practised to ruin her reputation (and with it sink her poor children to the lowest ebb of misery)" shows how deeply her mind had been injured. Like Miss More, she justified herself to herself, and her method was to empty the figure of her benefactress, in whatever shape it had appeared to her, of virtue. This alone could finally destroy her sense of obligation; and it was as part of this process that she derides with heavy sarcasm the maxims of cautious charity.

> Keep wretches *humble*, for when once reliev'd,
> They oft-times prove our *Charity* deceived:
> Therefore be *cautious*, nor their *merits* trust;
> They *may* have very few—if poor—they *must*.

> Think not a savage virtuous—but confine
> His future acts by obligation's line:
> He surely *must* be humble, grateful, true,
> While *he's* dependent—the superior you.

It was a rage that covered grief, and years later, refashioning her *Address to Friendship*, she suffered the grief to exhale. Once more she rejects Pity and Benevolence from the courts of friendship, and then the fierce lines slide into a wail of regret:

> Ye are the foes of Friendship! Your grand seal
> Is Grief insulted by Dependance. Those
> Who wear it, Friendship shuns. Oh ye have spoil'd
> My claim to that fair angel! I had fill'd
> My soul with plans that dignify; composed
> My spirit sick with frenzied passion; taught
> Sweet confidence, that strikes her stubborn root
> Downward with time, to own me!—This I did
> In noble fellowship of mind, and stood
> On my own base, weeping the ills of those
> Who call'd for wealth to cure them. I had none.

These fair hopes had been deceived.

The refashioned *Address to Friendship* was also rededicated, and its recipient was Ann Yearsley's second patron, Frederick Augustus Hervey, Bishop of Derry and Earl of Bristol. No stranger successor to Hannah More could be imagined than this cultured and able latitudinarian, kindly, a patron of the arts, a bad husband and father and, from her point of view, a pagan and a Sabbath breaker. He was in Bristol in the autumn of 1785, and he visited the milkwoman in her cottage and gave her £50, which she used to bring out a fourth edition of *Poems on Several Occasions*, entrusting it to the Robinsons, since Cadell, Miss More's publisher, had closed his account with her and refused to have anything more to do with her work. It was on this occasion that she showed him the torn fragment of the original *Address*, the only piece of writing she had by her. When her next child, a short-lived little boy, was born, the Bishop stood sponsor for him and suffered him to receive his name, Frederick. He gave her countenance and patronage, but chiefly he sympathized with her desire for education, and it is to this that she recurs with gratitude ten years later when she dedicates to him her *Rural Lyre*. Her other friends had discouraged her ambition as incompatible with a labouring life; the Bishop, on the contrary, heartened her to persevere.

She needed all the friends she could find. Financially her situation must have been somewhat eased, though, since she was not able to carry out her plan of opening a circulating library for some years, the profits of her first book must have been held in trust for her children, in conformity with her proposal to Miss More. In 1791, when her play *Earl Goodwin* was published, she still called herself a milkwoman, but early in 1793 we find her established in a circulating library at 4 Hot Wells Crescent, under the colonnade. Southey tells us that her shop was not upon a scale to prove attractive, but it was certainly in a good position. William Matthews, in his *New History, Survey and Description of Bristol*, sketches the busy life of the spa in the last decade of the eighteenth century. It had grown rapidly of recent years, and a gravelled parade, 800 ft. long and shadowed with trees, lay along by the river. Besides provision for invalid visitors, there was a well-developed social life; balls and assemblies were held in winter and summer, musicians played in the pump room, boats went down the Avon with music, and ladies and gentlemen crossed at Rownham Ferry to eat strawberries and raspberries with cream in the "sweet and wholesome village of Ashton". A little of this stirring life with its foundation of melancholy went into her poems, but not much; she was less interested in manners than in the human heart.

Miss More's biographer says that at Hot Wells Ann Yearsley was shunned and discountenanced, but though there is doubtless some truth in this statement, there is also some exaggeration. She had a party in Bristol. Her poems appeared in the *Bristol Gazette and Public Advertiser*, and Matthews, Bristol's historian, wishes her luck in a passage where her name appears in significant propinquity to that of Chatterton, "the

unhappy, but *scientific* and *valuable* youth". It was a parallel
that struck many—none more deeply than the milkwoman
herself, who claimed kinship with Chatterton as firmly as she
rejected it with the Poetical Blacksmith of Chilcompton and
such small fry—and they were unwilling to see it completed.
She had enough friends to account for a good subscription list
to the fourth edition of her *Poems on Several Occasions* in 1786
and to her *Poems on Various Subjects* in 1787, and enough friends
to bring her play *Earl Goodwin* to the boards in Bristol in 1791
and ensure its favourable reception by a "highly genteel and
numerous audience". Cottle was her friend and James
Shiells, who had intervened in her dispute with Hannah More,
was a beloved friend to the end of his life. Nor did the world
outside Bristol wholly reject her, though she never marshalled
again such a glittering company of patrons as applauded her
maiden effort. The interest of the *Monthly* and *Critical Reviews*
in her survived the publication of her *Narrative*, and they
treated her later works respectfully and at length. But her
position can never have been easy nor her manner conciliating.
She was not amiable. She lacked altogether the docile sub-
servience that makes charity a pleasure. Even before she had
formulated her instinctive reactions as social ideas, and had,
in the eyes of conservatives, become contaminated with
liberalism, she had gall to make oppression bitter. Among
the few facts that can be placed in the period between the
quarrel with Miss More and the opening of the library is a
dispute with Levi Eames, alderman and late mayor of Bristol.
The story is poured forth in the *Advertisement* to her *Stanzas of
Woe, addressed from the Heart on a Bed of Illness to Levi Eames, Esq.*
(1790). With intense resentment she tells how, in the hay
harvest of 1789, her two sons, the elder aged twelve and the
younger nine, playing with other children in Mr Eames's
field, were horsewhipped by his footman, the younger in the
field, the elder in her house, whither he ran for shelter.
Several nights later the servant gave the younger boy a second

dose, whereupon Ann Yearsley summoned him, only to find that he was defended by an attorney dependent upon the magistrate, who was Mr Eames himself, and that her own attorney advised her to drop the prosecution. For a year she digested her spleen; then, in June 1790, when she was carrying another child, she saw two boys chased by a servant down the same field; he failed to catch them, stopped and raged at Ann Yearsley. They were not, as it turned out, her children, but the fright and emotion brought on a premature birth, and the child died. She owed Mr Eames humiliation, serious illness, the excessive punishment of two children and the loss of another. The day that the physician allowed her to open her bedroom window, she began a poem, "the first offering I have ever laid upon the Altar of *Insolence*", as she declared in a provocative dedication. Heavy with denunciation and lament, vibrating with pride and anger, she hurled it at the head of the ex-mayor. But such weapons in the hands of the poor fall short or recoil. The hot wells, by which she came to live, were praised by physicians for their use in tempering "a hot, acrimonious blood"; but only time and death could slake hers.

With these iambics she published another poem, far happier but almost equally intense. In August 1790 she apprenticed her eldest son, William Cromartie, to an engraver; Cottle says that the premium was 100 guineas. To set his foot upon "the Grecian track" was a poignant triumph, for she was still ill, and thought she might not live to see the results of her efforts; but she begs him, when, after her death, he shall come to read her poems, to think her endeavour justifiable. He is the fair flower, born in the sunless shade of a lightning-stricken tree. She has read Shakespeare with him, and she prays that he may be the heir of virtue as well as love. She adds some touches of particular advice. He is to despise Jason for his treatment of Medea; he is not to be deluded by talk of the happy savage and the golden age, and he is not to be intimidated by custom, for: "Know thy spirit in *herself* must live."

Her own warfare with custom—that conflict of the naked with the impenetrable antagonist—cannot now be deciphered. One is sure of the war cries and the wounds, and sure that at some time the struggle was rendered more arduous by a love embraced in spite of prudence and admonition and painfully reduced within the bounds of honour. This conviction grows upon the reader who works through the *Poems on Several Occasions* and those *On Various Subjects* and is confirmed, nine years later, in *The Rural Lyre*. "I chose distress", she admits in a fragment of verse in her first book,

> And the sad bondage of resistless love.
> I knew the struggles of a wounded mind,
> Not self-indulging, and not prone to vice,
> Knew all the terrors of conflicting passion,
> Too stubborn foe, and ever unsubdued;
> Yet rashly parleyed with the mighty victor.

Beyond this avowal there is food for fancy but no solid substance for biography. Echoes of the parleyings of Ann Yearsley with her love strike confusedly through her poems. The object is never seen, unless he is the Rinaldo who gave her a silver pen and received in return a tribute to friendship, fierce with scorn of those who declare it impossible. There are many stubborn defences of friendship, retaliations on slanderous tongues, and angry rejections of advice. There is also a determination to keep this relationship "within the line of spirit". The consolation that she can offer him rises from sympathy in sorrow and must not be poisoned by passion. Along these perilous paths she reeled. *Lucy, a Tale for Ladies*, celebrates a chaste friendship, built on a passion that has been mastered, but brought to ruin by malicious tongues and the jealous tyranny of a boorish husband. Lelius dies of decline, and Lucy follows him.

She dies! and Cymon's poignant grief
Is finely wrought in bas-relief.
To prove he does his wife lament,
How grand, superb, her monument;
There weeping angels cut in stone,
The rose snapt off ere fully blown,
The empty urn—must surely prove
Cymon's deep sorrow, and his love.

John Yearsley, cast in this heart-easing poem for the part of
Cymon, perhaps never read the verse nor filled the role; nor
did Ann sleep under an emblematical tombstone. The tragedy
that played itself out in her imagination was a tragedy of
gentlefolk, who brood on their grief in what she recognizes
as "fatal leisure". The milkwoman sustained her mental
conflict as she sustained her daily task; tended her milk trade
first and afterwards her library, brought up her children and
started them in life, and so was able in the beautifully named
Remonstrance in the Platonic Shade flourishing on an Height to look
back at the path she had trodden and reassert her faith in the
real unity in trinity of love, friendship and virtue.

In this sacred shade,
Whilst cruel duty fettered every sense,
I saw my morning sun ascend with tears,
And sink at eve with heaviness; the night
Came burthen'd with despair; yet unsubdued,
I frown'd indignant on my chains, and tun'd
My rural lay to universal love....
I saw one mighty good, and wished it mine....
"Folly" could ne'er o'ertake me. Oft I verge,
When warm'd by fancy, to the farthest bound
My sense of words can bear; but at the extreme
Contemn the sense that chastity throws off.—
"Folly!" Good heaven! have I not climb'd an height
So frightful, e'en from comfort so remote,
That had my judgment reel'd, my foot forgot
Its strenuous print, my inexperienced eye

The wondrous point in view; or my firm soul,
Made early stubborn, her exalted pride,
Though of external poor; the stagnant lake
Of vice beneath, than Cocytus more foul,
Had oped its waves to swallow me, and hide
My fame for ever....I attained
With wretchedness this summit; hence, look down
On the lapsed ages, towers, and sleeping kings,
Whose heads repose mid monarchies engulf'd,
With temples, oracles, long whisp'ring fanes.

The burthen of despair, the stagnant lake, the ascent, the summit—these are to us stale metaphors, but to her they had their primitive freshness and force; no dust of libraries hovered between her and the scene she drew, and it is a fresh wreath that she brings so late in the day to Petrarch, without whose example

> what mind had dar'd
> To own that flame, kindled so near the throne
> Of God, it makes men like him?

This consideration will not deflect criticism, but will help the biographer to hear the voice of a living woman in these forgotten and imperfect lines. The vision of the last three, though it confesses, as so much of her work does, the influence of Young, does nevertheless record the release of the mind from the prison of self, through contemplation of the world in its winding-sheets of oblivion.

She had an imagination filled with time and eternity, and a naturally devout mind, strenuous but baffled in its intention Godward. In her first book she used Christian language; later she discarded it, and censured in Christian parable and iconography the "impious absurdity of human pride, in levelling ALL to human conceptions". On the wall of the hall of execution in her *Royal Captives* is painted God the Father, "an old man, sitting in judgment, cloathed with majesty, crowned with glory, and approving murder". She read history with disquietude, tracing through it the perpetual distortion of divine truth in the thought of man, and found herself thrown back on the unknown and unknowable God-head, of whom she could postulate only mercy. She cannot "pray at watch-words of mankind", but she can brood intensely on death as the gate of knowledge. Death is to her a point of vantage, an explosion of spiritual energy. Nature banquets the senses, but the spirit thirsts till it has found in death its cause. She does not, any more than her master Young, dwell on the circumstances of dissolution. It is a natural process, brushed aside by her characters, as they concentrate their energies in the face of the supreme change. Of a dying man it is said with defiant circumlocution, that he "yielded to Nature all she could claim from him". "All partial formation must dissolve," meditates the hero of the *Royal Captives*, in expectation of the death-stroke, "though the great system of Nature shall eternally renovate. Am I not, in the grave, the undoubted property of God?" The flash, the reversal of thought, the sudden shifting of scale and value, she learnt from Young; but the word is her own, and it is fine.

It was an unschooled and solitary mind that beat on these great questions. One kindly ear, however, was open to her. In the poem *To the Memory of James Shiells, Esq. Aged Sixty-Six* she tells how this good friend, who had already tried to atone the difference between her and Hannah More, would sit in her house, listening and gently checking her audacities. Could not the atoms of Chaos, she asked, have been the fragments of some decayed universe? And at night, shaken by this extension of imaginative vision, she lies sleepless in bed, listening to the Avon running by. The visit of Shiells, the sleepless night—they are almost the only scenes we have of her life at the Library. There is, however, one more, contained in the poem

Soliloquy, printed in *The Rural Lyre*. The poem is dated 27 February 1795, and is preceded by a little dialogue.

> *Author* (to her son). Go you to bed, my boy.
> *Son*. Do you write to-night?
> *Author*. I do.
> *Son* (laying his watch on the table). See, how late!
> *Author*. No matter—You can sleep.

This, we feel, happened. The boy's watch—it is a pleasant sign of comparative prosperity—did lie on the table as Ann Yearsley, after a day's work in her shop and house, sat down to write. She had probably intended to get on with the last volumes of her novel—the date fits—but the watch, ticking in the silence, drew her mind aside, and she yields to the impulse.

> How patiently toils on this little watch!
> My veins beat to its motion.

She begins, and is soon groping her way along dark lanes of thought. The abstractions, time and memory, the "corpuscular and mechanical philosophy" give place to the image of the dead friend, in whom that change is now fulfilled that must take place in her. Once more she considers death, tightening her hold, as she does so, on the dignity of existence; for, if loss of consciousness is final, she is still an atom of a grand whole. Here she checks her conjectures. "This watch is down." How can eternity be gauged by our "measured remnants"? So, in her time and fashion, Ann Yearsley came to "mark the skulls" as her mother had done before her.

The chief fruits of her years at Hot Wells were her novel, *The Royal Captives* (1795), founded on the mystery of the Man in the Iron Mask, and her third and last collection of poetry, *The Rural Lyre* (1796). The novel was her most sustained imaginative effort. The Robinsons brought out the first two volumes at the beginning of 1795 and the last two in April, and G. Robinson told Cottle that he had given £200 for the

book, which, if Cottle is trustworthy, is some evidence of the
continued vitality of her name in the publishing world, for
common novels were not bought after this rate. The two
important literary reviews, the *Monthly* and the *Critical*,
hastened to notice it, and nothing more generous or judicious
could be written than the *Monthly*'s critique. The sincere
energies of her mind, the insuperable deficiencies in her equipment are weighed one against the other; the crude planning
of the story, the frequent inflation of the style, the uncouth
metaphors that shoulder themselves into the prose are all
admitted, but the reviewer insists no less firmly on the force
of some of her incidents and characters and the robust texture
of her mind. "If the reader of these volumes has thought
before," the reviewer concludes, "they will lead him to think
again." The *Critical* spoke of genius, which was a word of
wider application in the eighteenth century than it is now, and
both reviews were certainly inclined to graciousness by the
liberal sentiments, the just abhorrence of tyranny which the
book reveals. The modern reader, unacquainted with the
singularly low standards of the novel at that time, will be
checked at the outset by improbabilities so monstrous, a
melodrama so naïve, that it can be approached only in a mood
of tolerant amusement. Advancing in that mood, he will find
himself stumbling on half-shaped fragments of invention,
grandly conceived, grotesquely executed, contorted by the
force of feeling that imagined them and the unskilfulness of
the brain by which they were developed; and among these
evidences of thwarted intention he may, like the *Critical*
reviewer, chance on sentences "which he cannot pass without
self-examination".

The book that Ann Yearsley wrote in the night, when she
had sent her children to bed, is ushered in by a preface in which
there mingles with the customary note of defiance a new note
of resignation. It seems to have been written at a time when
her work on the novel had been hindered by illness, and she

was not sure that she should ever live to finish it, for, after avowing proudly her desire for fame, she continues:

One of my motives for publishing the work unfinished, is that the world may speak of me as I am, whilst I have power to hear. The clouds that hang over my fortunes intervene between me and the public. I incessantly struggle to dissipate them, feel those struggles vain, and shall drop in the effort.—This consolation I shall bear with me to the verge of life, that, to those that have guided me by the sacred and lambent flame of friendship, my memory will be dear; and that while malice feebly breathes, truth will boldly pronounce.

Let the faults of this performance, the Gothic extravagances, the clumsy imitations of Sterne, be admitted at once and without extenuation; and let the reader's mind be free to consider what the woman who wrote that preface was really trying to say.

The book begins in a shadowy tumult of mystery, chains, endurance and death. We hear the suppressed agony of the prisoner to whom poison has been administered—"Deadly draught! Bitter!—Bitter to an extreme!"—and the clamour of his friend; a soldier passes "in whose countenance were discernible the tumultuous traits of unfinished murder"; a Cordelier enters the cell to shrive the prisoner. Then the scene melts, unexplained, and we follow the hero through "a subterranean passage, arched and glittering with webs full of unwholesome droppings". It is a hundred pages before a coherent narrative begins to emerge, and many more before Henry, exploring his island prison by night, descends a broken ladder to find himself "not on pavement, or polished marble, but on human skeletons, whose bones were white as ivory with age", where, leaning on a coffin, he finds his lost father, a royal prince, the Man with the Iron Mask. The involutions, the recognitions, the misunderstandings and shadowy wanderings of the characters in search of each other, are not worth following. The Man with the Iron Mask had filled much space in the press of the early nineties, and Ann Yearsley, pre-occupied with tyranny and suffering as women writers often are, saw in the story a theme that would include her strongest feelings and her customary meditations. It also enabled her to express a sensational imagination of which there is not much evidence in her poems. She had responded with enthusiastic gloom to the *Castle of Otranto* when Hannah More lent it to her, and now she builds her own castle and constructs—though without any aid from the supernatural—her own mysteries. She had, perhaps, no perception that the living birds of her mind were nesting in stage scenery, unless it is at the end of the book where the lives of Henry and the fair Emily, of Henry's father and rediscovered mother are diverted in an arbitrary way to an unlikely happy ending, while, as a sop to history that knows nothing of such an escape, Dormoud, governor of the prison, is left behind to wear the Iron Mask.

It is in the characters of Dormoud and of Emily and Henry, who are his prisoners during most of the book, that Ann Yearsley's meaning lies; not that they are real as characters, but that they express, often incongruously, her mind and experience. Dormoud is, indeed, an effective figure in his simple kind. Cold, polished, debonair, voluptuous, not coarsely cruel but quite unscrupulous and self-interested, he is an artist who takes pleasure in the ironical effects his position enables him to arrange. He has some compunction for the unconscious Henry, as he sits at supper with him on the night ordained for his death, but more satisfaction in his own skilful ambiguities and in the tremendous scene that he explodes on his victim as they reach the Hall of Execution: "You have been faithful to my friendship, useful to my love, and loyal to my Sovereign—So, Sir, kneel—Executioners, do your office." To such a pass comes the soul that excludes feeling; and rightfully is that hypocritical visage encased in an iron mask.

Dormoud is the foil to Henry, the ardent and suffering human heart, that will not pervert its God-given energies, but glows with noble rage against the oppression it sustains and with enthusiasm for the beauty revealed to it. Like many of her generation, Ann Yearsley scorns the human being who represses in public the rich emotions of the soul. Experience was for her always passionate, and emotion, though not the whole substance of human intercourse, was its indispensable medium. Cold tranquillity she called the grave of thought, but the passions were the wings of spirit. It is not, however, feeling alone, or even chiefly, that distinguishes Henry and the austere maiden Emily, whom he loves; it is that they continually try to trace and understand their feelings. This analysis, at once rational and lyrical, strikes the reader oddly in a Gothic novel. One recognizes again the sequence of themes—pride, questioning resentment, and the effort to appease it by the contemplation of some vast process of time—which had been the subject of her lonely meditations. The ashes are still hot. "I sickened with ingratitude; I grew impure", she writes, and cries out, perturbed, at the industry of the imagination in fomenting grief. Other familiar notes reverberate, struck by the same strong and venturesome hand. She is still deeply concerned to find beauty and satisfaction in unfulfilled love, and to contrast it with "the dull certainty of possessing" in marriage. None the less, "the fame of women *is found only within the pale of order*...it fills the lonely hovel with confidence and peace". In the grave Emily she embodies the fortitude that is the root of virtue, and the "refinement"—the word seems to stand for purification and sharpening of mind, will and emotions—that was her moral talisman. Her most interesting remarks are on solitude; not the mere forgoing of companionship, but the profound self-absorption of the soul, beyond the soundings of speech or even of articulate thought. In this final retreat she endured the apathy of misery, which, like Charlotte Brontë, she dreaded, but accepted as an inevitable phase of experience. Here was the matrix of that creative brooding, forced on her by the "gloomy and despotic power" of her own nature. Here was the mountain citadel of her assailed mind. In her allusions to this voiceless solitude there is a curious impatience with words. "To arrange words, make them trip after each other easily, and call a multitude of them Eloquence, is very pretty", she writes. "But oh! when the soul sits high amidst her stubborn virtues; when she braves the arrows of an injurious world; language, beneath her, is as the murmurs of a rivulet." Elsewhere it is "a shepherd's bell, heard from afar and forgot". This scorn of words is rather the unconscious concealment of her incapacity than a mystical transcendence, for she never attained full mastery over her instrument. Not that her prose is without merit. She has sallies of nervous speech, sardonic brevities not usual in the literature of the time, due, perhaps, in part to the peasant tradition, but in part the result of choice, for "condensed keenness" of expression is a quality that she admires, believing it to denote a nature "capable of enjoying happiness...in an exquisite degree". Thus Emily meets the jealous insults of her lover with the one word: "Base!" Here, however, we are already on the verge of rhetoric, and in rhetorical passages her love of the forcible often misleads her. Like Charlotte Brontë, she relished strength, and strong words are dangerous to her. "Revel", with its implications of easy power and exuberance, is a favourite ("Resign that picture", cries Henry's father, "or the richest stream that revels near my heart shall be wasted on your pavement") and "reciprocal", a word both economical and dignified, is worked hard. "Lambent" and "chart" adorn many passages, and so does "latent", which to her meant deep-rooted. There is something pleasing in her enthusiastic acquisition of diction, though it leads her to perpetrate, in her poem on the slave trade, not only "inky sire" for a negro father, but "dingy youth" for a negro son. At her best she achieves a collocation of new words that is like a chord, struck suddenly by a child fumbling on the piano. The poison carried to the prisoner is "a pale liquor, which seemed to congeal... with its own somniferous properties". Of the emphatic words in this phrase "pale" alone is likely to have been part of her inherited vocabulary; the others she discovered, a treasure trove. The same uncertainty of touch affects her imagery. Images came thick and fast to her, and she discarded none; some she did not pause to envisage properly, or she could not have entreated Fortitude to bid her little son "sit on Truth's most rugged point"; but from the blurred paragraphs there emerge at times significant shapes. "Behold", she writes, "how the fine-spun web of philosophy...strains with its load of human woe"; and, with one of her too rare allusions to her former life, describes the contented ox chewing his cud in the midst of flowers, "enjoying Nature like a lazy god".

In 1796 the Robinsons brought out her last collection of poems, *The Rural Lyre*. The book was adorned with a frontispiece, drawn by William Cromartie Yearsley, in which Liberty, strongly resembling Mrs Siddons, sits under the British oak, while in the distance we perceive the Trojan legions of Brutus. The book is wider in scope, more sustained and regular in verse, less uncertain in style than either of her earlier collections. It is also more impersonal in treatment and calmer in tone. In the dedication to the Bishop of Derry and Earl of Bristol she speaks of ill-health, care, the claims of business and the lack of leisure, but these obstructions have not prevented the development of her mind, while the near view of Hot Wells society, with its feverish and unprofitable activity, has gone far to reconcile her to poverty for herself and her sons. In the *Royal Captives* she wrote of a finely bred woman, forced to live for years the life of the poor: "Much did she deserve commendation, who could prove, that the soul can command her fate by submission, finely blend the magnificent with the minute, and act sublimely with feebler minds, so

delicately, that the latter shall draw comfort from the unison."
It is not very lucid writing, but the tenor is clear, and the sober
energy of the *Rural Lyre*, the cessation of the painful outcries
that ring through the earlier period, suggests that she had
made this effort herself.

The book begins with a long fragment on the landing of
Brutus, a specimen in the epic style of a subject which she
wished some poet would lift to rivalry with the *Æneid*.
Leaving this undertaking to a less encumbered hand, she
passes on to the gay society of Hot Wells, sketching with contempt the hunting woman, who neglects her baby to follow
sport, and with compassion the unmarried mother, stealing to
visit her child at nurse in the country, and distressed by the
rusticity and vulgar vice of his surroundings. There is an elegy
on Lord William Russell, suggested by her historical reading,
an indignant poem, more in her old vein, on the Bristol riots
in 1793 when the bridge tolls were reinforced, and a realistic
description in the *Captive Linnet* of the doom that falls on a
forsaken nest, the raids of the weasel and the voracious columns
of ants. There are also three odd poems, linked in a Roman
setting, familiar epistles in an easy, rapid blank verse, which
together form a moral idyll, wherein "the principle of self-
correction" is enforced by a wise old market woman, who, as
she binds the yellow legs of the pullet that her young master,
the Consul C. Fannius, has bought, obliquely reproaches him
for his pursuit of Nisa, the young wife of Tellus, the camel
driver. The eighteenth century had its own way with the
Romans, and, though startling, it is not unprecedented to find
Cato the Censor stroking a sickly kid, and camels on the
Sabine Hills. Ann Yearsley craved for the classics, but they
came to her diluted by translation and further altered upon her
palate. Her best touches are always homely and veracious to
the point of crudity. In *Clifton Hill* she had recorded the
screams of excited milkmaids, designed to catch the attention
of a passing man; here it is the loud laughter of Tellus's mates,

ready with their loads, and gathered in the early morning under the young husband's window to shame him. In her *Bristol Elegy*, when she speaks of the men who were killed when the military fired on the mob, she has a moment that recalls Crabbe and the unknown authors of old ballads, and A. E. Housman. The old mother waits in ignorance for her slaughtered son, while

> For him lies cooling on her narrow board
> His frugal supper in a single plate.

It is a pity she gave us so little of this genre painting and so many personifications; Goldsmith and Crabbe would have been better models for her than Young; but she was ambitious, and tried to look through and beyond her narrow environment. Miss Seward compared her once with Burns. Without caring to follow up so unequal a comparison, we may wish that current forms of poetry had been as friendly to her passions and meditations as they were to his; but popular poetry in England was neither capacious nor dignified enough to receive what she wanted to say, and the highly formalized couplet and blank verse required a more firm and delicate touch than she could give. *The Rural Lyre*, which presents clear evidence of an advance in style and verse as well as substance, proves also that in these forms she could never overtake her lack of training. It is certainly unlikely that her poems will ever be republished, and indeed the reading public has no need of them. Therefore, since it is of some moment to this study to record the level to which her unsparing effort raised her art, I have transcribed here three of her maturest passages. The first is from her best sustained poem, *The Genius of Britain, On the Rock of Ages, recommending Order, Commerce and Union to the Britons*. It is an ideal presentation of the British seaman, set against a background of primitive tribes, such as the travels of Cook and other adventurers had made familiar to imaginations at home. The Genius of Britain speaks:

                              Oft my son
Stray'd o'er the world of ice, his golden hair
Pendent with glittering rubies. On his breast
He wore my emblems: manners boldly firm
Conceal'd his heart dissolving: on his tongue,
Unversed in flattery, Freedom, born of Law,
Sat ever, to the Pagan yielding much,
Lest charity, philanthropy, and love
Should blush for his defect—Unfinished man,
Produc'd when Nature dallied with employ.
Maids taught to ride presuming waves, or snatch
Invaluable Zimbis from her bed
Transparent, lov'd my son. Mild dwarfish tribes
Mourn'd him; a ship-wreck'd stranger as he rov'd
Deep vales of Afric, gathering as he went
Fair truths of intellect, that blaze the mind,
Irradiate mem'ry, and instruct your babes,
When on the floors of Albion. From his form
Gigantic to their view the pigmy maids
Fled trembling; yet with insect skill contriv'd
Nets for his hair, rare sandals for his feet,
Canopy of light rushes, so contriv'd
By secret means, such as true friendship finds,
To consolate the awful rover.

At the other extreme from this sincere magniloquence comes
a vigorous sketch of a nursemaid, getting even with her little
charge, now that they are away from the parents' eyes.

I saw the beauteous Caleb 'tother day
Stretch forth his little hand to touch a spray,
Whilst on the green his drowsy nurse inhal'd
The sweets of nature, as her sweets exhal'd:
But, ere the infant reach'd the playful leaf,
She pull'd him back—His eyes o'erflow'd with grief;
He check'd his tears—Her fiercer passions strove,
She look'd a vulture cow'ring o'er a dove!
"I'll teach you, brat!" The pretty trembler sigh'd—
When, with a cruel shake, she coarsely cried—
"Your mother spoils you—everything you see
You covet. It shall ne'er be so with me!

Here, eat this cake, sit still, and don't you rise—
Why don't you pluck the sun down from the skies?
I'll spoil your sport—Come, laugh me in the face—
And henceforth learn to keep your proper place.
You rule me in the house!—To hush your noise
I, like a spaniel, must run for toys:
But here, Sir, let the trees alone, nor cry—
Pluck, if you dare—Who's master? You, or I?"

Finally I quote the first two verses of a poem, embedded, as the
Gothic fashion was, in her novel. It is derivative but melo-
dious in form, and not derivative in feeling. It shows her
lyric work at its most pleasing; the pitch is not quite sustained
in the later verses.

Wander!—nor pause within the haunt of man;
   The brook and bramble yield repast to thee,
Whose soul has formed her solitary plan,
   To whom wild nature yields her region free.

The rising sun is thine, the sultry noon,
   Grey-footed morning, and the evening star;
The midnight shadow, when the silent moon
   Half-horn'd on ending space, is seen afar.

With the publication of *The Rural Lyre* Ann Yearsley passes
out of the literary world. It was not widely reviewed, and the
tragedy, which she tells her patron that she hopes to revise
and publish, never, it seems, appeared. The domestic troubles,
which now fell upon her, were probably the chief cause of her
silence, but another may well have been that she had identified
herself with liberal sentiments and could no longer, in this
time of growing reaction, expect a fair hearing. The literary
criticism of the Tory organs was becoming deeply tainted with
political prejudice, while by the end of the century the liberal
reviews, that had praised the milkwoman's just hatred of
tyrants, were forced to step very warily. *The Royal Captives*,
with a plot based on the abuses of arbitrary power, was a
conscious indictment of absolutism; *Earl Goodwin* had been

launched against the superstitious zeal whose joy is persecution; and throughout her work there are strong appeals against the unjust portion that society allots to women. It was this last offence, by no means the least heinous in Tory eyes, that caused the Reverend Richard Polwhele to class her in his poem *The Unsex'd Females* (1798) with those who followed Mary Wollstonecraft.

> And Yearsley, who had warbled, Nature's child,
> 'Midst twilight dews her minstrel ditties wild,
> (Though soon a wanderer from her meads and milk,
> She long'd to rustle, like her sex, in silk)
> Now stole the modish grin, the sapient sneer.

Polwhele was a friend of Hannah More's, but not, on this showing, inveterately hostile to Ann Yearsley. She is deluded by self-love and Mary Wollstonecraft, but his are tones of admonition not rejection. His business is "to recall her, if possible, from her Gallic wanderings—if an appeal to native ingenuousness be not too late; if the fatal example of the Arch-priestess of female Libertinism have any influence on a mind once stored with the finest moral sentiments". On Mary Wollstonecraft, living and dead, he had no mercy; but Mrs Yearsley had remained, however rebelliously, within the "pale of order", and might perhaps be scared into repentance by the Arch-priestess's sad corpse.

Ann Yearsley died on 8 May 1806 at Melksham in Wiltshire, in her fifty-fourth year, and was buried four days later at Clifton. The tragic incidents of the last years of her life are variously reported. Cottle tells of the death of her eldest surviving son, the engraver, which must have been the stunning blow, and adds that that of a second son soon followed. "Ann Yearsley, now a childless and desolate widow, on the produce of her library, retired, heartless, from the world, and died many years after, in a state of almost total seclusion at Melksham in Wiltshire. An inhabitant of the town lately informed me that 'Ann Yearsley was never seen, except when she took her solitary walk, in the dusk of the evening'. She lies buried in Clifton Churchyard." The Reverend H. Thompson, Hannah More's biographer, deepens the shadows. "Her two sons perished in the flower of their youth—one in battle, the other by disease; and, outcast, desolate, and broken-hearted, she retired to her native town of Melksham in Wilts, where, in 1806, she died insane and destitute." On the other hand, John Evans, Master of the Academy at Lower Park Row and afterwards at Kingsdown, in *The Ponderer*, a series of essays which he contributed originally to the *Bristol Mercury* and published separately in 1812, praising her stern dignity of character, says that it accompanied her through every situation and enabled her "to breathe her last sigh in peace in the bosom of her family". Clifton Church registers make it possible to correct some of these statements and to trace tentative lines of connection between others. Melksham was not Ann Yearsley's birthplace, but it was close to Trowbridge, a centre of the woollen trade, where her third son, John, was in business as a clothier. As he survived her until 1814, when he died at Trowbridge and, like his mother, was taken to Clifton for burial, she was not childless, and as a stone was raised over the grave it is unlikely that the family was destitute. The registers are silent about the history of her daughters, Ann, born in 1782, and the oddly named Jan (Jane?) Jones, born in 1784; nor do they record anything of Charles beyond his birth in 1780. If Thompson was right and one son died in battle, it must have been Charles. On 10 March 1799 the burial of William Cromartie is entered. This can hardly be Ann Yearsley's brother, for there is no mention of more than one, and both she and Miss More speak of him as dead. The entry may conceivably be a mistake for William Cromartie Yearsley, the beloved son on whom she fixed her hopes. He would then have been twenty-two. We have, however, no evidence that he died in Bristol; no struggling poetry survives to tell us whether she sat by his death bed. One other entry concerns her. On 25 September 1803 her husband, John Yearsley, was buried, and it is natural to assume that the date marks the end of her life at Hot Wells. She left her buried hopes and followed her living child to Trowbridge.

Into the seclusion of her last years we cannot look, nor decide upon the nature of that state that Cottle calls desolation, Evans peace, and Thompson—but he wrote long after the event and his testimony need not be taken very seriously—the insanity of a broken heart. The lonely walks at twilight are convincing and characteristic. "Surely, solitude is the soul's home!" she had written in the *Royal Captives*; "she has no other; even when her finest energies go forth in love and friendship; and by placing her happiness in the power of others, she robs herself; yet she pursues that happiness by the strength of imagination; and loves the shadow never to be overtaken; till finding her folly too late, she returns to solitude and reflection." When she wrote this, she was contemplating solitude as a state of healing and reinvigoration, from which the soul, that "has been used to contemplate Nature on a general scale", must issue, to taste of pleasure once more and combat pain; but if the power of self-renewal were exhausted, it would be to this state that she would make her final retreat.

Her death produced an unkind epitaph, which is cited here as evidence that she had not wholly sunk into obscurity.

> Ann Yearsley tasted the Castalian stream
> And skimmed its surface as she skimmed her cream;
> But struck at last by fate's unerring blow
> All that remains of Ann is—"Milk below".

Some brief revival of interest prompted the re-engraving of Miss Shiells's portrait of her in 1814 and its publication in the March number of the *Ladies' Monthly Museum*, and in 1831 Southey, a Bristol man, treated her with sympathetic respect in his *Lives and Works of Uneducated Poets*. Since then her name has fallen from few pens except the hostile ones of Hannah More's biographers.

The writer once saw in Canterbury the earliest Christian burial ground temporarily uncovered. There were no relics, but in the clay were preserved the outlines of the uncoffined figures, and especially that of a shrouded woman with a new-born child in her arm. It is in some such shape as this that Ann Yearsley is present to the imagination. In her painful births she could not impart life, and nothing remains of her poetry in the sense in which alone poetry can be said to live; but we can see where she lay.

THE SCOTCH PARENTS

∧∧∧∧∧∧∧∧∧∧∧∧

IN the novel of the second half of the eighteenth century
a visit to the theatre is a not uncommon incident. The
locus classicus is the fifth chapter of the sixteenth book of
Tom Jones, where Partridge fails to admire Garrick's Hamlet,
on the grounds that he himself, if he had seen a ghost, would
have looked and behaved in just the same way. Miss Evelina
Anville also went to see Garrick and responded more sensi-
tively to his naturalistic art, and it is very often in Drury Lane
that the heroine of the minor novel is enabled to give those
convincing proofs of sensibility that endear her to the
hesitating hero. She sits in the side-box, a Cinderella from
the country, intermittently conscious of fine feathers, and
it is this part of the house that novelists most frequent;
occasionally, however, a picaresque writer accompanies his
bumpkin or his rogue to the gallery and takes a place near
Partridge. Here, at Drury Lane and Covent Garden and
sometimes at the Haymarket, a rougher London took its
pleasure, imbibing emotional and declamatory tragedies,
staring down at magnificent architectural settings, roaring at
farces and exacting servile apologies from defaulting actors.
We do not get very near to this section of the audience, except
through the glass of the satirist or the complaints of the
disturbed playwright, but one odd and unedifying pamphlet,
scum of an already seething press, does preserve the lineaments
of a playgoer of this rank. During October 1772 "John

Ramble" took Nell Macpherson ("Eleonora"), to whom he ought to have been married, once a week to the play. On Thursday, 6 November, they went together for the last time, perhaps to Bickerstaff's ballad opera *The Maid of the Mill* at Drury Lane, but more probably to Covent Garden, where they could see the first performance of *Henry VIII*, not acted for twenty years, with Bensley as Wolsey, Wroughton as Buckingham, Mrs Hartley as Queen Katharine, and the coronation of Ann Boleyn in the fourth act. They returned to Ramble's house in Pimlico, and a day or two later Nell was removed by her family, and the young man was left to contemplate his truncated romance, which he did to such purpose that by 2 May 1773 he was able to send Nell's mother a printed copy of *The Scotch Parents: or, the Remarkable Case of John Ramble, written by himself, (in the month of February, 1773). Embellished with elegant Copperplates of the singular and uncommon Scenes contained in this Narrative,* together with a note in which he promised to stop publication if, within two days, Miss Macpherson were returned to him as his lawful wife; otherwise he would publish to convince the world who was most culpable, parents or children. No answer came from Mrs Macpherson, that "rigid presbyterian", and on 4 May the disappointed lover sent to the press a copy of his note and an explanatory letter to his readers and had them added to his book. "Now I may venture to affirm, I have done my utmost for my dear Eleonora Macpherson," he wrote, with an agitated superfluity of commas, "and my conscience is clear—Now, may God and man, act towards these Scotch parents, and myself, as we merit." In a few hours he stood before the world.

No bookseller had risked a penny on Ramble's remarkable case. The *Monthly Review* gives Bladon as the publisher, but this appears to be a mistake, for the title-page states that the book was "printed, and sold by all the booksellers in Great Britain and Ireland"—which means that it was the author's venture. Reviewers took little note of it, and, indeed, to a literary judgment it is so much waste paper, the production of a vehement, ill-balanced, ill-educated mind. The author suspected its deficiency "in point of scholastic rules", but relied confidently on the value of his material, and this, it is true, may arouse ten minutes' curiosity, for it has some psychological and some historical interest. It is interesting that the book exists at all, that Ramble expressed his undisciplined emotions not in ballad verse, the traditional utterance of the people, but in a detailed prose narrative. This was the result of the growing popularity of the novel. Contemporary satirists show us the milliner's assistant fetching thumbed volumes from the circulating library. Nell Macpherson was a milliner's assistant, and she and her lover stood well within the shade of that "evergreen tree of diabolical knowledge". But a stronger influence was the tragic Muse of Drury Lane and Covent Garden. Upon his title-page Ramble put a quotation from Garrick's version of *Romeo and Juliet*, where Juliet in the tomb revives in time to enjoy the parting scene with Romeo of which Shakespeare deprived her. Garrick had acted this scene but had now handed the part over to younger men, and in October 1772 Dimond was the Romeo at Drury Lane.

> Parents have flinty hearts, no tears can melt 'em—
> Nature pleads in vain—children must be wretched,

quoted Ramble, equating himself complacently with Romeo, and in this tone he told a great deal of his story. Whenever possible Nell is Eleonora, and he and she—but particularly he—speak a tragic jargon, ungrammatically dovetailed into their natural speech and moving in a sort of battered blank verse. These playhouse echoes contrast oddly not only with Ramble's natural vulgar English but with all the scenes and incidents he has to describe. We see two things equally sharply, Ramble and Nell as they were and as he liked to pretend they were; and we hear two notes, the usual speech of eighteenth-century Londoners of the shopkeeping class and the strained and throaty rant which was their conception of the heroic. How far Nell entered into this fancy world it is hard to say. She went with Ramble to the theatre, and may have been at once subservient and intelligent enough to conform to the style; but it is most often her remarks, keenly real in accent, that have defied alteration. Ramble set it all down, her unforgotten flightiness and amorousness and his own morose passion and poltroonery. He did not conceal, he hardly even dignified, the shops and inns and lodgings in which their love was conducted. Strengthened perhaps by the parallel of *George Barnwell*, a drama that ventured into the counting-house, he found all these circumstances sufficiently apt for tragedy, and as to his own fitness for a tragic hero he had no doubts at all. The result is a complete self-exposure, but, as he had neither humour nor irony and had not inherited any traditions of politeness between the sexes, he did not perceive his nakedness. For him the proof of his manhood lay in his capacity for passion, in having been the victim and the tyrant of Nell Macpherson. His motives in writing, he declared, were to redeem his honour, to express his love and to show the world that extraordinary incidents happen sometimes in a middling state of life; and without any misgiving he proceeded to "lay before the public the proof of what men and women can do when they love". He wrote under a pseudonym and changed the names of all the characters in his story, which must have hampered the efficacy of his revenge. An identification has been proposed, but it will be most convenient to consider it as a sequel to Ramble's self-portrait.

John Ramble, then, comes before us as a young draughtsman with a taste for music and the theatre; he handled a guitar and wrote verse, which he set and sang. In summer 1771 he was living in lodgings "near a market not far from St James's. Being at that time clear of all connexions whatsoever, happy in having no particular tie on my mind and heart; everything

was alike agreeable." One of the shops in the market was kept
by a Scotswoman, Mrs Macpherson, with a daughter Nell,
"a young lady remarkable for her personal accomplishments".
There were some other children and a father of disconcerting
character and ambiguous occupation. Ramble says vaguely
that he "lived with a person of distinction", and one suspects
the flunkey, especially when one hears of his accompanying
his master into the country; but later he appears to be a builder
or bricklayer. He was not amiable, "never speaking to his
wife or children but on absolute occasion, never giving the
least assistance towards maintaining the family". At present,
however, he remains behind the scenes together with the rest
of the Macpherson family, for, though Ramble went to look
at "this fair creature who lived so much in men's report", he
could not get up spirit to enter the shop and address her,
"her looks bore such unusual dignity"; and he left London
for the west of England without exchanging a word with the
girl. On his return home in the winter he missed her from the
shop and learned that she had gone out prentice to a French
business near Grosvenor Square; for some time he could not
trace her, until one day, looking for new lodgings in that
neighbourhood, he had the door opened by Nell herself in a
"French night-cap". He was rather struck, he says, with a
certain air of melancholy that hung over her. Plainly she
recognized him, for she stared at him with a mixture of surprise and pleasure as she asked his business. He took a room
in the house. The leisurely prelude of his love was over, and
the tempo quickens.

The first movement was flirtation, carried on in the friendly
atmosphere of the milliner's household. There was Mrs
O'Trimmer, the milliner, her husband, her mother, Mrs
Donaldson, three or four apprentices, a forewoman and a maid.
Ramble sang and played to them on his guitar, praised Nell's
voice ("She sung heavenly") and kissed her in the passage.
He took her, with her father's permission, to a concert and

noticed with some disquiet—for he was quickly jealous—that she would not take his arm and continually looked back at a gentleman who followed them. It was the first note of discord, faint as yet, but disturbing. He repeated the kiss, observed that *she resisted not*, but refrained from breaking his mind to her. Chance, however, overrode his reserve on the spur of physical pain. He fell downstairs while carrying his guitar, was helped up and comforted by Nell, and, thus stimulated, made a declaration which was kindly received. He did not trust her. When she went home that evening for the week-end and declined his company, he followed her and saw her escorted by a " gentleman " or " young fellow "—he uses both terms. Confronted and reproached on her return, Nell explained that her companion was her uncle. She also explained that the ring and watch she wore were the presents of a female cousin who had gone to Scotland. Ramble has enough crude artistry not to anticipate his catastrophe. He still passed many pleasant hours, and his narrative reflects them. When Nell was at home during the week-ends, his muse produced songs " to mitigate the pangs of absence ", and she, in graceful acknowledgment, changed the white ribbon on his guitar for a pink one. It was not until March 1772 that he received clear proof of her perfidy. They were walking in Bond Street, and " in one curs'd distractive minute . . . a person met us, and without any ceremony took her by the arm, and in a very singular manner began upbraiding her ". It was a young German, Heslebourg or Hesselbourg by name. Ramble resented the rudeness with some spirit, arranged a meeting for mutual explanation and walked his false charmer away, leaving his rival " cursing his stars in a shocking manner ". He was in a very strong position; Nell loved him and he had proved her fickle; he proceeded to establish his ascendancy in his own way.

At this point Ramble's class becomes an important condition of his story, for he was not gentle either by nature or breeding, and no suggestion of chivalry shaped his behaviour to his sweetheart. In Maurice Hewlett's *Wiltshire Essays* an attempt is made to distinguish between those ballads that originated with the peasantry and those that originated with the gentlefolk by their treatment of certain themes, especially that of love. The sensuality of the former is more brutal in its circumstance; it is not restrained by any convention of manners and has no terms to keep with the graceful. However that may be—and Sir Graelent, who impounded the bathing lady's clothes, was the hero of an aristocratic audience—*The Scotch Parents* is certainly a class document. Ramble took every advantage that the situation offered, without remorse, and does not seem to feel that any excuse is called for on this point. He embarked upon a series of scenes in which the vehemence of his encounters with Nell was nicely balanced by the tameness of those with Hesselbourg. At first Nell met his reproaches with spirit, crying: "Tell him he's a villain if he says I ever gave him liberties." Then the iambic cadence is heard, and we see her on her knees invoking plagues and torments on her soul if ever she forgets her Ramble or deceives his faithful heart. Ramble hinted eloquently at his possible death in defence of her honour, and used her agitation to exact grotesque pledges of fidelity from the miserable girl. He was prepared to forgive her by inches and pass her through a sequence of graded tests; and for the first of these—"Let me have liberty to take a lock of hair from what part of your body I please." He had his will and reciprocated the gift, and Nell closed the scene with unexpected elegance by binding her neck ribbon about his arm. The reaction followed immediately; she knew that she had put it in his power to ruin her, and she spent the rest of the evening brooding "in a disagreeable state". Ramble retired and made his will, with some ruptures of grammatical concord, but impressively enough, since he left her all his property.

The meeting with Hesselbourg, however, hardly justified

such preparations. Both gentlemen were sufficiently moderate in their behaviour. Hesselbourg, who was the "uncle" of a former occasion and the giver of the ring and watch, told Ramble that he had received "modest liberties" from Nell; but he had no claims to press; he had got over his infatuation and was prepared to be sententious over the fickle young woman. "She cannot go on long in this guilty manner," he meditated; "it's not every man will behave with so much honour as I have done: and then she'll meet the infamy she deserves"—a prophecy of which Ramble does not seem to perceive the full bearing. Hesselbourg showed him love-tokens of Nell's, letters and flowers of her workmanship, and thriftily asked his supplanter to get his ring and watch back for him. The interview closed innocuously. Nell was left to the tender mercies of her surviving lover.

When he got home she followed him up to his room, to be met with a stream of abuse. "O thou cruel creature!" raged Ramble, "now where's your vows? You've given up your honour to make me believe you? Where's your thoughts, when you sent me with a burning lie in my mouth! to confront this Hesselbourg?" She cried out that she was lost, since he hated her, but for some time stood to her main point, that she had never given Hesselbourg liberties; yet she shrank from confronting the slanderer, and by the evening—it was a long and stormy day—she had been brought to admit "some liberties" but was still insisting that she had never really loved him. She had left him for Ramble, whose lost opinion she undertook with tears and prostration to regain. Ramble, certain of her instability, but moved by a confession so much in his favour and quite unable to leave her, let it go at that. "I took the pink ribbon off my guittar till the time came that was to convince me of what she had promised." He took the ring and watch back to Hesselbourg, who acted as a cynical chorus to his rival's story; Nell, he told him informatively, had had many offers, honourable and dishonourable, and he specified one lover of the second class, a Scotch gentleman, Galloway by name, living near Berkeley Square. Here was more food for Ramble's jealousy.

The next stage of the story is dominated by the white ribbon, which hung over Nell like a sign of wrath and estrangement, to be removed only by an abasement of devotion. Her first effort was to bring him a signed pledge of her love, which he transcribes.

I, Eleonora Macpherson, swear that I love John Ramble faith-fully, and have consulted my heart, and find that it is in my power to confine all my wishes to him for *ever*; and that no fleeting thought, towards any other man, shall *ever* pass from me. I am his, and only his: no man but him (so help me Heaven) shall ever possess my body: and in case I should be so lost to love, virtue and gratitude, as to neglect the same John Ramble for any other man: may he by the following confession, have it in his power to ruin me.—I have granted him every liberty a woman could grant a man, no part of my body have I denied him to see and touch; Likewise have I taken the same liberties with him.

To this confession I put my name, to satisfy the same John Ramble I am his—(having lately deceived him) and sooner than lose him I love, I would condescend to every thing he could desire.

As witness my hand and seal

Eleonora Macpherson.

This is my Act and
Deed, April 2nd
1772.

Ramble records the scene with a rich effusion of rhetoric; he was indeed considerably impressed and agreed that the docu-ment might "stand as a memorial of woman's love for ever", but he would not yet replace the pink ribbon on his guitar; some "extraordinary deed" was still required of Eleonora.

Two days later, on 4 April, they went a little way out of town together on a solemn jaunt; and here Ramble turns aside to sketch a domestic tragedy, also connected with Scotch parents. He did not like the Scotch at all; he scatters gibes at them throughout his book and at one point transcribes a letter from Will MacClack, Nell's uncle, a vigorous but illiterate performance, in order to "shew his sentiments, qualification and learning, of which Scotland prides itself so much". The presumption behind his title is that English parents would not have behaved with such barbarity as the Macphersons, and he hails the opportunity of exhibiting in the Donaldsons the same national trait. The victim in this case was Nell's employer, Mrs O'Trimmer, who had married against her parents' will, had been unhappy, and now lay dead in childbed in a lodging-house outside town. The unforgiving parents, according to Ramble, refused to see her, and he sets down Mrs Donaldson's presence in her daughter's house simply to thrift; she was keeping an eye on the business. He and Nell went, however, and on the way back Ramble was seized with violent toothache and found himself unable to walk further. They went into a public house and asked for a room, and here Nell's emotional sympathy made her an easy prey. "There was a bed in the room. . . . Situations at *times* are so critical that it is not in the power of us mortals to resist." That night she came to him in his room; and one expects to hear after this that the pink ribbon was restored; but it seemed to Ramble that the time was not yet ripe.

By this time the Macphersons had got wind of his attentions and Nell was sent for to come home. "I went with her", writes the impassioned lover, "as far as her mother's, but did not go in, fearing I might not be a welcome guest." When he was admitted to the Macpherson household—for the parents were not harsh and hoped their girl had prudence enough to look after herself—he must have cut a poor figure there, for though tolerably shameless he had not the good fortune to be brazen. He and Nell made no difficulty of hoodwinking the mother, who was a "rigid presbyterian, neglecting everything for her religion", but the father was more formidable, and Ramble was "never very happy in his company. He would indeed in a sneering way ask me how I did; and afterwards, if I stayed ever so long, would never take notice of me. I could not bear it; if he had liked my connexions with his daughter, he would have behaved more civil; if, on the contrary, he did not approve of my being with her, why did he not tell me so, not treat me with such contempt?" Neither man pressed for an explanation, and Ramble generally managed to keep out of the way. He took Nell out for walks and to Covent Garden and to see the pretty new houses near Buckingham Gate, one of which he contemplated taking, "as I really had honourable intentions towards my Nelly". She tried to please him by working for him, "doing everything the most humble, slavish creature in the world could do for hire", he says with triumph, and then remembers a more graceful phrase and praises her "lovely, modest condescension". At times, however, "a very stubborn behaviour" blemished this humility and brought out the brute in him. One evening in Hyde Park he struck her several times and followed up the blows with reproaches. She turned from him in despair and went towards the Serpentine River, resolved "to rid me of her stubborn soul. . . . I, willing to see how far she was in earnest, let her go on." He lost sight of her in the twilight, experienced, one hopes, a pang of disquiet, and overtook her on the brink, with torn hair and her face swelled with tears. There were ejaculations and a reconciliation.

He took no further steps towards marriage and evaded Mrs Macpherson's inquiries as to his intentions, but in his tortuous mind he seems to have meant to marry her one day, if she proved herself a wholly satisfactory partner. In order to facilitate the proof, he made the proposal, which even he admits to have been foolish, that she should set up a millinery business in part of the house in Pimlico, which he had now acquired; he would then have had ample opportunity to judge of her disposition without finally committing himself. He had seen many young lovers marry in ignorance of each other's characters, and was not minded to court disaster that way.

In August they had another violent scene. Nell was still at home and had promised her jealous master that she would keep out of men's sight, but it came to his ears that she had been seen shelling peas in the shop with her mother. That afternoon they went to drink tea at Kensington, and he did not speak a word the whole way there. At the tea table the girl at last ventured to ask what the matter was, and thus led up to the premeditated outburst of his stoked fury. "Determining to terrify her a little", he caught her by the throat, and accused her of being in the shop and of making no effort to leave home again and go back to work. "Where's your boasted resolution, your pretended courage now?" he jeered. After this the scene soared to great heights and must be described in Ramble's own dialect, in which, more closely than usual, we hear the transition from fact to fancy.

The tea things being brought in, she uncovered the pot, and without any ceremony put her finger in the scalding water.—See, she said, if I have any resolution,—let this convince you: and if I this morning neglected to use it, the next occasion I will despise everything, sooner than you shall have cause to blame me again, here shall my finger stay till you take it out; here shall it suffer till the water's cold, if you think I deserve any punishment for what I have done.—I instantly took her finger out, and willing to have further trials of her constancy, I cried, this is all art,—I will see whether there is need of the resolution you pretend. Upon which I put my finger in, and saying (quite otherwise than what I felt) this is nothing—thou false deceiving devil!—I hate you!—you make my life one continued scene of misery—I will now be revenged on you for all your plagues to me, taking up a knife, and throwing her on the bed, I roared out, now will I search that heart of yours and see whether it is foul or spotless.

O Ramble, she cried, with an irresistible look of love and terror, will you kill your Nelly? Can you have the heart to do it? O change those frowns, kill me not with them, smile but on me, and then strike this faithful bosom, which then will bleed with pleasure, since it is my dear Ramble's will to see his Nelly weltering in her gore—if he can have the heart to kill me.—Kill you! I cried, I will sooner tear my soul, and dam myself to all eternity than hurt you! Thus, thus will I murder you (taking her in my arms) and send your soul to heaven: and there, in a pleasing ecstatic agony of consummate bliss, die on my Nelly's bosom, and follow her to the *realms of undescribeable delights*, and then be repayed indeed for all the torment we now have suffered.

In the intervals of these exercises, Ramble was enthusiastic about his Eleonora; and it is plain that she was by now violently in love with him and deeply subservient—willing to beat her treacherous head against a wall if it could entertain a thought to his prejudice. Her final testing was near, and circumstances—he would not stick to say Providence—worked in his favour. Towards the end of September Ramble was established in his house in Pimlico, had let off part to an Italian and his wife, "clean, sober people", and had hired a little girl to do the work. In the Macpherson household it was known that the O'Trimmer business had changed hands, and the question was, was Nelly to be "turned over" with it? It was now that Ramble began to press Nell to broach the question of their marriage with her father. He disliked the thought of the undertaking himself, and, as he points out, it afforded Nell an excellent chance of proving her constancy. It was pusillanimous conduct, but girls of Nell's class are accustomed to bear a good deal of the responsibility of love-making, and Nell accepted her task, though with misgivings. Together they wrung a number of suitable emotions out of their suspense; and then, one morning at the beginning of October, at six o'clock, Ramble, lying in bed, heard a loud knocking at his door. The Italian opened it, and Nell came running upstairs, wet to the skin and carrying bundles. Her father had not forbidden their marriage, she said, but he had refused her any help. "It's out of my power to give you anything, you've been expensive enough to me already." So she had told her mother that she was already married, had packed up her clothes and come away. She poured out the whole tale to Ramble, as he lay there, and then pulled off her wet cloak and threw herself down by him on the bed. She had come for good, she declared; she now cast herself upon his love and mercy. "I made her no answer, but got up directly, and then put the exiled ribbon on my guitar, and shewing it her, I said, look here.—You remember the token."

Nell was satisfied with the gesture. She was in a fine romantic glow, and responded to his renewed promise of marriage in the terms of the Nut-Brown Maid: "I could bear to see you married to another, and spite of my sex's pride, wait on you both"—or so Ramble says. He could not, however, hope to satisfy Mrs Macpherson with a pink ribbon, and he tried to stave off trouble in that quarter by telling her, when she came to see them, that they had been married on 4 April ("the day I enjoyed my Nelly"), but as he was obliged to refuse her any other information, her tardy suspicions were not appeased. "You never yet was Man to say to me what you intended towards my Child", she remarked unanswerably, and went away leaving Ramble apprehensive of a suit at law for marrying a minor. His apprehensions were strengthened a day or two later when he met Mr Macpherson and Mr Donaldson, the subsidiary Scotch parent, in the street and they spoke "forcible truths" to him there. He went home and wrote a letter, acknowledging the facts and promising marriage when Nell came of age; and, full of resentment at Mr Donaldson's participation in his affairs, he added a lofty counsel of discretion. But, though he might swagger with his pen, he was seriously disquieted and, as usual, could think of no measures but evasion. He and Nell left the house and "rambled about with aching hearts, uncertain of being long together" and absorbed in thoughts of death and parting; at twilight they crept back from their miserable wanderings to have their suspense relieved by Mr Donaldson with the practical message: "Get married as soon as you can, and there will be fifty pounds for you." But Ramble, sure once more of his ground, was not to be cheated of his heroics; he added up his grudges against the Macphersons, brought up the total with their offer of money and refused magnificently to be bribed; he would not bear it to be said, he writes, that he married Nell for fifty pounds. After this manœuvre, except for an unpleasant and inconclusive interview with Mr Macpherson in the street, the lovers were left alone.

Ramble's spite, the induced sensations of injury and revenge with which he covered his humiliations, were now directed solely against Nell's parents. Now that she herself was continually under his eye, his jealousy was calmed and, contrary to likelihood, he makes an idyll of their few weeks together. These were days of fair weather, clouded only by Ramble's occasional "melancholy fits". There were no storms in or over tea-cups. A chastened and proved Nell settled down in Pimlico, discharged the hired girl and undertook her work with a resigned condescension that made Ramble "silent, praise his maker". She also contributed to his progress in art, and he embellished his book with a portrait of her (this I have not seen; it is lost from the British Museum copy) and an amateurish study of the nude, labelled: "Miss Macpherson In the Character of one of the Graces sacrifising at the Alter of VENUS." Once a week he took her to the play, and for six weeks they were very happy. His conscience was at ease, for he was still contemplating marriage, though, as he pleads, some time was required to surmount his natural reluctance at the thought of marrying his mistress. Indeed, the only feature of his domestic arrangements that seems to him to demand explanation and apology is the garb that Nell wore at her housework. It was thrown up against him later by her family as an example of meanness, and he goes through it piece by piece. "Next to her shift (for it was seldom I could prevail with her to put on her stays) she wore a white silk waistcoat of mine; over that a red flannel one, and then a blue jacket, made from a coat of mine, a round-eared cap, and on her feet slippers." It sounds sluttish, but Nell may have given the odd dress a negligent charm. It was in this attire that she was found when her relations came to fetch her away.

For now the scene darkened. Nell became the prey of frightful dreams of separation and woke crying in his arms. Feeling that Heaven might be forewarning them, Ramble determined to marry her next week and put an end to their fears. But his resolve came too late. On the threshold of misfortune he appeals to his readers for sympathy and makes his only admission of misconduct. "Remember with moderate anger", he adjures, "my great fault in ruining Nelly, and delaying to marry her till now.—Call to mind the delicacy of marrying a Girl too soon after the loss of her honour. Forget not what proofs I have given all along of a faithful unchange-able passion for her"—and much more to the same in-tent.

On the afternoon of Friday, 7 November, the parents, "beasts in the shape of human creatures", sent to Pimlico a Mrs Drulin, a poor relation of the family, with the story that Mr Macpherson was dying in Bath and that Nell must go to her mother. By this means she effected an entry, and in her rear followed the illiterate uncle MacClack. They meant to take Nelly and take her alone, and had provided themselves with assistance from "the proper people". There followed an elaborate scrimmage, for Ramble, though very little martial and mightily afraid of the law, did at least cling to Nell, invoking death, until his arms were benumbed with the blows of the assailants. A young gentleman, who arrived at this moment for a drawing lesson, seized MacClack by the collar, but Mrs Drulin cried out that Nell was her daughter and that the villain Ramble had got a wife and three children, and he withdrew from the ambiguous conflict. The crowd that had assembled was unhelpful—Ramble was perhaps not a popular neighbour—and presently Nell was wrenched from her lover's arms, dragged to a waiting coach and lifted in.

I, all fury and madness, rushed towards the coach, and had got my right leg and thigh, and part of my body in—Nelly laid hold on me, and cried, O let him come with me—have pitty on us.— MacClack being above me, beat me on the head, and stamped on my thigh, till at last I dropped on the pavement deprived of motion, and before I recovered they drove away.

It was veritably the end; he did not see her again. He made vain enquiries at her mother's house, and then retired to nurse his bruises, indulge "shocking thoughts" of Nell's fate, and pity his enemies for "being unable to feel the Godlike attribute of sweet mercy". On Sunday Mrs Macpherson called, demanding angrily whether he would marry Nell, but Ramble, finding his mind divided between love and honour, answered her evasively, and, after giving vent to all the native fury of her soul, she left him. He was unfortunate in timing his scruples, as presently appeared when, on reflection, love triumphed and, from the bed to which emotion and injuries now relegated him, he sent this note to Mrs Macpherson:

Ma'am, I have that to propose to you, will make us all happy, from

J. Ramble.

"When I sent this", he adds, his enormous vanity still unshaken, "I never imagined but I should meet with a ready compliance to what I desired." Mrs Macpherson's reply was a rude awakening; it was too late; her daughter had gone where Ramble would never see her more. Ramble was deeply shocked. How could a mother refuse a chance of restoring her child to virtue and happiness? Surely Mrs Macpherson's religion must cover some hidden enormity, since she was so uncommonly unnatural as to turn a deaf ear to his offers. An interview with the implacable woman had no better results, though Ramble burst into tears at sight of the parlour where he had so often seen Nell; nor was a letter to Mr Macpherson at Bath more successful. Different rumours came to his ears; Nell had gone to Scotland, to her relations; she had been sent to a convent in France; she had gone into keeping by her own and her parents' consent, "they concluding, if she must be a whore, to be one for something". There was also the possibility of her death. All his clothes had been returned to him immediately, except the silk waistcoat that Nell had worn next to her shift; he imagined her clinging to that as long as her strength lasted, and when that too was returned he was able to see in it a fatal significance. He put on black, misquoted Hamlet, wrote a "Cantata" and two airs, alluding to his unfortunate situation, and set them to music. He hoped the next world would recompense him for his loss in this. After Mr Macpherson had returned to London, Ramble made a last effort and went to visit him, with a relation in support to help him plead his case. When the interview proved fruitless, he gave up hope. He was not deprived, however, of the pleasures of rhetoric. He imagined his Eleonora in "a dreamy, Cloystered cell", and assuaged his grief by composing a handsome soliloquy for her and equipping it with suitable stage effects—Gothic gloom, the hollow notes of a tolling bell, an open grave. "Soon", cries Nell, "shall I become the sheeted tenant of such a place as this. . . . I feel my soul subdued—and my debilitated frame submits itself to the attacks of gastly (sic) Death—which, as all hopes of Ramble are at an end, I will welcome. . . . Yet Oh! I am afraid, in spite of my heavenly abode, I shall be unblest without my Ramble." From this flattering performance he turned to provide himself with alternative apostrophes, one to Nell considered as "a Martyr to Truth and me", the other in case she should now be "revelling out the guilty hours in wanton luxury"; and with that he concludes the necessary defence of his honour. No doubt the composition had in some measure allayed his pain.

Maurice Hewlett, pursuing his quest for ballad origins, decides that *Lord Thomas and Fair Annie* has "all the characteristics of the peasantry, naïveté, mother-love, sentimentalism and realism". Mother-love does not enter into

The Scotch Parents, but it is true to Hewlett's other marks. It is naïve to a degree that wakes a strong ironic reaction in the reader; it is minutely realistic, especially in its dialogue, which is detailed with all the unnecessary circumstantiality of the uneducated; and its sentiment is copious, unrestrained and has the obliterating quality of that which gushes for highway-men and murderers, as Hewlett illustrates in his essay *Catnachery*. Yet another strain, that of tawdry romance, is not to be found in the early ballads; it was the symptom of a more complex state of society. The wine of the older romantic drama, adulterated with spectacle and coarsened to the taste of the time, frothed up in the rough cup of the theatre to the lips of the gallery; and the theatre provided a fancy-world then as the cinema does now.

"A ridiculous, low, ill-written story", sniffed the *Monthly* reviewer, adding nevertheless that Ramble's account had, to give him his due, throughout the air of *truth*. An egoist too crude to serve Meredith as theme, too low to be paired with Fanny Burney's admirable Mr Smith, too destitute of courage and ingenuity to win more than a disgusted glance from Fielding, Ramble must yet be heard when he pleads with his reader to remember that *The Scotch Parents* was "wrote by the person who *really suffered*". His suffering was all of his own manufacture, but it seems really to have occurred. A possible identification of Ramble is suggested by a manuscript note on the title-page of the British Museum copy of *The Scotch Parents*, one of Sir William Musgrave's books. It runs: "Mr Carter, son of a Statuary in Piccadilly." This would be Nichols's "honest John Carter" of the *Literary Anecdotes* and *Illustrations*, the draughtsman and enthusiast for Gothic architecture, whose *Pursuits of Architectural Innovation*, a series of papers in the *Gentleman's Magazine* between 1798 and 1817, called attention to the surviving specimens of ancient building up and down England and did much to prevent ignorant dilapidation. A brief search has revealed nothing that conflicts with this identification and many facts that support it. In profession, tastes and temperament the two figures agree.

John Carter was born in 1748, the son of Benjamin Carter, marble carver, of Piccadilly. He left school at twelve, with an education so imperfect that everything he wrote is blotched with misspellings and grammatical inconsequence, but he had already evinced a taste for music and the drama that accompanied him through life. The instrument he played at school was the flute, not the guitar. He had already begun to compose, and at some time of his life—the obituaries are not precise as to dates—he set portions of Shakespeare's plays to music and composed two romantic operas on mediaeval subjects, for which he designed the scenery. His taste for ancient monuments developed early and he began, before he was twenty, to explore various parts of England during the summer months, taking sketches of mediaeval sculpture and painting. (This habit would explain the journey to the west of England that interrupted the courtship of Nell.) He applied himself closely to his craft, supporting himself in his early years by work in a surveyor's office and by superintending workmen engaged on buildings. The dates that mark his emergence into the public eye fall later than 1773; it was not until 1774 that he was employed to draw for the *Builder's Magazine*, the Society of Antiquarians took him up in 1780, and in the same year he began to publish his *Specimens of Ancient Sculpture and Painting*; so that an impression of him at the age of thirty, some five years later than the events recorded in *The Scotch Parents*, is perhaps as near as we can draw to Ramble. "At that time," we are told, "Carter was reckoned an odd, close man, and supposed to have saved some money." He died a bachelor in 1817, in Upper Eaton Street, Pimlico.

His character was idiosyncratic, and even the friend who writes over the initial "B" in the eighty-seventh volume of the *Gentleman's Magazine* does not try to make it appear amiable. He was temperate, frugal ("even to parsimony" according to another witness) and capable of enduring hardship, and his integrity was incorruptible; but "his manners were reserved; his temper irascible; and his resolution sometimes bordered on obstinacy". He had an odd trick of representing himself as alone in the world (Ramble too describes himself as "clear of all connexions whatsoever"), though actually he had a brother and sister living, as well as other close relatives, at the time of his death. He had the reputation of a quarrelsome man, and his writings, particularly when he attacked the despoilers of ancient buildings, were full of severity and sarcasm. "He felt the premeditated attack upon these objects of his veneration", says one writer, "as an attack upon himself, as if his own rights were being invaded," and his friend "B" remarks: "He would repeatedly declare himself a '*coward in everything but the good old cause*'; and this I sincerely believe, for exclusively of this he had no fixed determination: nervous to an excessive degree, he would fancy the greatest consequences to have arisen from the most casual and trifling cause; and a dispute with a servant has brought on a fever." It is not necessary to point out how closely this calm and by no means unfriendly analysis corresponds with the fervid self-exposure of Ramble. It is true that there is not anywhere in *The Scotch Parents* any allusion to Gothic architecture; the branch of his art that is occupying Ramble is drawing from life; but to set against this there is the fact that the style of Carter's contributions to the *Gentleman's Magazine* is exactly similar to that of Ramble's more elevated passages in its ungainliness, its unhappy attempts at fine writing and the violent energy of its rhetoric. There is even the trick, learnt from bad dramatic blank verse, of using an adjective where prose prefers the adverb. "I retrospective saw"— writes Carter, and Ramble had declared that Nell's housewifery made him "silent, praise his maker".

I have found no conclusive evidence that Ramble was Carter, and no indication of the source of the attribution in Musgrave's copy of the book; and it is perhaps unnecessary to labour very hard to bring home to an honest though disagreeable craftsman a discreditable youthful amour. One may think, if one accepts the identification, that Nell Macpherson's warm beauty did for a time take precedence of Gothic sculptures in his mind, and that her withdrawal finally riveted him in the chains of his own oddity and reserve. It is certain that he died in Pimlico and possibly in the house from which Nell had been dragged forty-five years before. Between these two events, he did a good deal of useful work, often in an awkward and offensive manner, was made Fellow of the Society of Antiquaries and consulted by Kemble on the dresses and decorations for his Shakespeare productions. He made some fast friends of long standing, including Nichols, and he cheated the expectations of his relatives by sinking all his money in an annuity and dying before he received the first quarter. He applied his stormy emotions and his obstinacy where they did some good in his generation; to him the spire of St Michael's, Coventry, was a "soaring gem", while modern "alloy, neglect and mutilation cast a loathsome mist" before the heritage of ancient workmanship. This was a respectable and tenacious passion, though he did not always manage it well; Nell Macpherson's lover had become, as the *Gentleman's Magazine* called him, "Antiquity's most resolute friend".

CLIO IN MOTLEY

ΛΛΛΛΛΛΛΛΛΛΛΛ

PARODY in the eighteenth century is not always a form
of disrespect, nor is its appeal, *pace* Dr Johnson, always
that of a momentary triumph over the grandeur that
has hitherto held the mind captive in admiration; it is sometimes a salute and sometimes the avowal of a guarded and
apologetic liking. To the first kind belong the mock-heroic
poems with *The Rape of the Lock* at their head. These are no
reductio ad absurdum of the epic formula, which emerges un-
scathed, since the true heroic is unassailable and the forms in
which Homer and Virgil expressed it safe in the reverence of
generations; nor does the satire often bare its teeth against
the modern world, foolish as some of its manifestations may
be. As the heroic befitted the plains of Troy and Latium, so
the unheroic befits Augustan England; the coffee-mill turns
at Hampton Court and the grateful liquor glides into the
china cups, and this is as admirable in its place as the sacrificial
meals, the roasted carcases on which the fighting men by
Scamander nourished their brawn. Behind the brightly
painted scenes of modern life the epic shadows loom benignly.
The epic forms are filled with incongruous material; and the
result is not ridicule but a piquant disharmony; we contemplate two dissimilar forms of excellence in surprising juxta-
position. The same method, the same sort of effect, though
less defined, is found where the object of the parody still stands
in the washing tides of opinion; where the poem is Chaucerian

or Spenserian or Miltonic; but here the model is more questionable, and in following it the parodist has also submitted it to a test. The accidental charm of distance is withdrawn, and the older poet is haled out of the twilight into the full rays of reason and the present. What of Milton survives Phillips's cider vats, what of Spenser comes untrounced from Shenstone's schoolroom, may be held to be established. What has been tested is the range of a poetic voice, its carrying power in unfamiliar circumstances.

Parodies like these breathe a cautious friendliness, far short of surrender, or they hide under a bluff conceding air some warmer enthusiasm. With these we must classify the three burlesque romances of James White, *Earl Strongbow: or, the History of Richard de Clare and the Beautiful Geralda* (1789), which is ostensibly concerned with the Norman invasion of Ireland, *The Adventures of John of Gaunt, Duke of Lancaster* (1790), which narrates the apocryphal adventures of four sons of Edward III on their way to a tournament at Carnarvon, and *The Adventures of King Richard Cœur-de-Lion* (1791), which traces that hero's return incognito from his Styrian prison. These books are quite unlike the gloomy and melodramatic performances of the historical novelists of this decade. James White keeps terms with the Age of Enlightenment, and his concessions are large and gay. Nothing could be handsomer, from the standpoint of reason and fun, than his embarrassed knight-errant, rescuing a reluctant damsel eighteen years after her abduction and riding off with her while she sticks pins through the joints in his armour. But this is less than the whole story, and one has still to ask why James White wrote books in which men wore armour and rode on quests; and the answer can only be, because such images were dear to his imagination.

Little is known of James White. He is not to be confused with Lamb's friend, Jem White, the author of *Falstaff's Letters*; his career falls earlier. The obituary notice in the

European Magazine for April 1799, on which we have to depend
almost entirely, calls him a graduate of Dublin University,
and this is borne out by the *Catalogue of Dublin Graduates* which
records a James White who was a scholar in 1778 and a
Bachelor in 1780. He was probably Irish, and he wrote himself
Esquire on his title-pages, which was then a claim to gentle
blood. His first book, a translation of Cicero's *Orations against
Verres*, was published in London in 1787, and for the next
twelve years he seems to have passed his time between London
and Bath, where he had "respectable relatives". He was well
known in the literary world as a scholar and translator, and
critics were almost consistently kind to him. The space
between his graduation and 1787, however, is not filled in.
There is among the sonnets that Dr Downman wrote to his
friends, to accompany copies of the 1781 edition of *Poems to
Thespia*, one addressed to James White, Esq., that touches on
the theme of flight, so characteristic of our writer. When the
collective mind of states is poisoned by luxury, writes Downman, and falls into ignorance and vice, "insulted taste"
retires from the vile capital to the distant provinces, where
nature and virtue are still valued and where the poet can write
for a public whose judgment is not yet depraved; but the last
line is ambiguous and suggests that the recipient of the sonnet
was a patron of poets rather than a poet himself, and there
were demonstrably other James Whites in the West whom
Downman might have addressed. We are thrown back on
White's books, in which certain recurrent themes suggest
experiences clear enough in their nature though, naturally,
indefinite in detail; the most important of these are the poor
clerk and the treacherous friend, and they are generally, though
not invariably, linked together. The poor clerk is handled
farcically in the figures of the two "ushers" of noble damsels
who in *John of Gaunt* exchange their miserable and moderately
comic confidences at night in the robbers' camp. Ungainly
young fellows of humble birth who have compassed a little

learning, they are exposed to the mockery of their noble charges and the spite of the servants; their damsels titter at their rustic pronunciation and the servants lay booby traps on the stairs. Far more dignified is the figure of Claribert the minstrel, to whose counsels Earl Strongbow yields an almost filial obedience. Here we have the whole range of the situation as it lived in White's imagination, conscious genius obstructed at first by poverty and then by envy, but receiving at last the honour that is its due from those few capable of comprehending it. Each of his heroes has a minstrel in attendance and pays him respect; John of Gaunt and his brothers are accompanied upon their adventures by Chaucer himself, who is the brain of the party, and though the great achievement of Fitzherbert, the rescue of his King from captivity, is over before the *Adventures of King Richard Cœur-de-Lion* begins, amends are made to him in the last pages of the book, where Richard founds a mixed order of knighthood to include scholars and minstrels, and appoints him to a place in it.

Claribert, then, has encountered envy, and envy, coming to light as treacherous friendship, as the scorn of the prosperous and stupid for the shabby and intelligent, is very much in White's mind. It has one of the marks of an obsession in that it intrudes unexpectedly into contexts in which it has very little relevance. Thus the Countess of Salisbury warns young Strongbow against the jealous man who will conceal his vice under a show of friendship, brood in delight over the imperfections that intimacy enables him to perceive in his victim, and finally expose them to the world; but no such fate befalls Strongbow, and the warning remains a detached piece of resentful satire. The rhetoric which this theme evokes is far more substantial, more full of particular instances, than that of White's other tirades; Claribert's version in his account of his life is particularly elaborate. He was the son of an honest potter in Rouen, and as his "stateliness of mind", the sign of genius, was mistaken for a pride unsuited to his origin,

it called down on him the malice of his social superiors,
especially of those just above the line of trade. He had to
endure "sly barbarities beneath the garb of facetiousness" and
to perceive too late that his false friends had prevented him
from approaching patrons of real benevolence. These attacks
he met with disgust, hatred and contempt. "Ignorance and
envy", he says to Strongbow, "have, in every age and clime,
debased the human species. The 'Son of the Carpenter' was
reproached at Nazareth." The allusion is startlingly incongruous and obviously sincere, and this sudden drop of the
voice on to a note of deep seriousness is one of the characteristics of White's style. He had opinions and sentiments
and unhappy haunting grudges, and when these occurred to
him, even in the gayest medley of his romantic burlesque, he
uttered them without reserve through whatever fictitious
mouth was then open. It is thus the epicurean robber-chieftain,
Raymond of the Bushy Beard, who unexpectedly expresses
White's horror of the modern young atheist. To Claribert he
gives some part of his experience, however refashioned, and
perhaps exemplifies in him what he hoped might be his own
fate. Stung with slights, the minstrel betakes himself first to
travel and then to retirement, storing up wisdom in solitude
and emerging at times to inspire some noble youth, like
Strongbow, with the love of virtue. "From his temperance,
his love of exercise, and constitutional hilarity, he lived to a
venerable old age." The hilarity was perhaps constitutional
in White; the fun and whimsicality of his books do not sound
forced; but the melancholy obsessions were constitutional
also. For a while they hung in precarious equilibrium; then
the balance was overset.

The history of Claribert had not sufficiently purged White's
smarting sensitiveness, and in his next book *John of Gaunt* we
seem to detect other parts of his experience. Chaucer is a poet
honoured as poets should be. At Woodstock, in surroundings
idyllic with gardens, meadows, a porch overshadowed by white

jessamine and a hospitable kitchen, "did the independent and happy poet lay the groundwork of immortality". But even Chaucer speaks tartly about the state of the drama, on which he disdains to employ his pen, and he is supported by the abbot of Shrewsbury, whose monks have found their careers as dramatic writers obstructed by the favouritism of the "directors of moralities", the debauched state of public taste, the evil influence of critics who aspire to be playwrights and the "cowardly, occult and malignant jealousy" of the modern man of letters. Less than fifty pages further on, the obsession lifts its head again in the confession of the anchorite. This story is particularly revealing. The anchorite had been a young aspirant for literary honours, who had accepted the help of a man superior to him in mind though inferior in rank or fortune. After a while the contrast rankled, and the young man engaged in the manœuvres of the envious. He gave his friend bad advice; he indulged in the "spurious sincerity" of reminding him of his faults; under cover of hospitality, he assailed the unguarded guest with impertinence. But the friend was neither blind nor helpless. His forbearance was exhausted, and with a few verses of exquisite ridicule and severity he drove the ingrate, convicted of guilt, from the literary world to the anchorite's cell. Part of this story, one feels sure, White believed to be his case; the other part is a compensating dream of power and vengeance. Such thoughts were the strange substructure of his burlesque. They hardly intrude at all into his third romance, the sunshiny *Cœur-de-Lion*. Genteel poverty is there, and snobbery, and the extreme importance of clothes, but as sources of mirth only; the bitterness has been drawn out of them. It seems, as one turns the pages of this book, as if the evil spirit has been exorcised.

White's three burlesque romances appeared close together, between 1789 and 1791. Before that he had published in 1787 a translation of Cicero's *Orations against Verres*, and in 1788 a shilling pamphlet, *Hints for a Specific Plan for an*

Abolition of the Slave-Trade and for Relief of the Negroes in the British West Indies. In the interval between the two first novels came *Conway Castle; a poem* (1789), and after the third he returned to translation with a version of the *Speeches of M. de Mirabeau the Elder, pronounced in the National Assembly of France*, 2 vols. (1792), and of St Étienne's *History of the Revolution in France* (1792). The strongest link between his books is the passion for oratory that they express. Oratory, to this contemporary of Burke, Sheridan, Grattan, Flood and Mirabeau, is one of the great instruments of social and political justice. "It is this two-edged eloquence", he wrote in the preface to his translation of Mirabeau's speeches, "which kindles up the ardent and persevering spirit in great assemblies, elevates the public soul, leads to virtuous revolution and purifies political society. It is this which discomfits court-favourites, overthrows administrations, seats integrity at the council-table and gives capacity her due place." He published his version of the *Verrine Orations* with an eye to the impending trial of Warren Hastings; the allusion was obvious and he was not the first to make it; for a year before the trial began, supporters of the impeachment had seen Hastings as Verres and Burke as Cicero. Hastings appears again as Longchamp, Grand Justiciary, Chancellor and Papal Legate, at the end of *Cœur-de-Lion*, where his tyrannical exercise of delegated power and his escape in female apparel from the Tower of London provoke the ornate eloquence of the "intemperate and exclamatory" Lord Geoffrey Fitz-Peter. Longchamp's exculpatory speech is ingenious, and he faces the indignity of his disguise with great spirit, citing Hercules and Achilles and reminding his audience that, as an ecclesiastic, he was partly in petticoats already; but White sees to it that he is pretty thoroughly exposed. His arguments—"I went upon the grand scale of expediency," "If it was an outrage, it was a patriotic outrage," and, defending magnificence as a necessity of state, "The multitude must be dazzled"—are hostile comments on the defence of Warren Hastings; and the trial ends, as White wished the real trial to end, in the disgrace of the accused.

There is a great deal of public speaking in the three romances; indeed, they are largely shaped by this master-enthusiasm of White. They move from harangue to harangue; their situations are mostly such as invite formal oratory, and where they do not obviously invite it, the oratory is nevertheless to hand. In *John of Gaunt* the four young princes-errant, passing a night in an oak tree, overhear the conversation of two ladies on palfreys below, and take occasion to discuss the ethics of their enforced eavesdropping, thus "improving their understandings by salutary debate, and laying in a stock of polite and genuine eloquence". Polite and genuine eloquence is, in truth, not easily hampered by circumstances. The rounded periods stream surprisingly through the keyhole to which the Lady Barbarina's lips are applied, and from the mouth of the famished friar whom the Black Prince and his brother wind up by pulleys from a dungeon. Cœur-de-Lion, in particular, is as doughty with his tongue as with his sword. It is he who expounds to the Lady Ursulina the case for swearing, as honourable to the saints whose names it keeps in fallible human memories, and maintains his point in quick-fire, dialectical cross-talk with that formidable lady; it is he again who inflicts upon the Duke of Saxony's daughter a towering rebuke, in which the culpable unconventionality of that "stubborn, preposterous, unparalleled maiden", in declining to be rescued from a caitiff who has for years been her accepted lover, is enforced in an orderly sequence of paragraphs, knit together by the emphatic refrain: "Holy St Anthony, what a damsel!" Best of all, however, White likes oratorical set-pieces, the formalities of proposal, seconding and amendment, the decent but acid references to the noble baron who spoke last and the venerable prelate who disgraces the woolsack, the cries for "Order!" and the intercalated retorts below the swell of moral adjuration. Some such scene he arranged in each of his romances. Ancient chronicles, he remarked, while preserving records of plagues, insurrections and famines, had omitted parliamentary discussions, and he set himself to fill the gap. *Strongbow* culminates in a full-dress debate on the siege of Wexford, during the earl's invasion of Ireland; *John of Gaunt* sweeps suddenly up to the Border and a wholly apocryphal battle with the Scotch, in order that there may be occasion for a similar display, while *Cœur-de-Lion* includes the proposal to impeach Longchamp, and sets the scene in a Westminster Hall familiar to the eighteenth century, the seats of which are crowded with ladies who have come to hear the *fine speaking* and weary before the end.

These wilful anachronisms are among the most enlivening parts of the romances. The first unmistakable extended passage of this nature is the debate on the siege of Wexford, where, one after another, Fox ("an able Knight of a fleshy habit of body", characterized by "the tendency of his hue to brownness and an extensive pair of very sable eyebrows"), Sheridan ("a tall and slender Knight...the inditer of many joyful ballads and...Moralities", whose easy shrug and slight lisp are "not ill-adapted either to his flippancy or to the polished sneer and quiet sarcasm that sometimes mingled in his orations") and Pitt ("a young man of a stiff neck and great probity, the extreme erectness of whose position was not a little increased by the lofty station he had held") rise to their feet, tuck their helmets under their arms and launch into full parliamentary eloquence. As we consider the unexpected appearance of the faithful Commons of George III against a twelfth-century background, we are constrained to ask what they are doing under the walls of Wexford. What sort of book did James White imagine himself to be writing? What game does he play?

His game, though he was not fully aware of it till towards the end of the first romance, was the masquerade. He delighted to consider the past and knew, compared with other historical novelists of his decade—Sophia Lee, for instance, or Ann Fuller—a good deal about it. He knew how tourneys were conducted, and that ropes and a pulley were often the only means of exit from mediaeval dungeons; he knew the names of the ancient Anglo-Irish families; he knew that mediaeval ladies travelled in waggons with creaking wheels, and that it was their function to unarm and wash the warrior. He made mistakes; he thought that a wandering knight would be able to borrow a suit of mail from a well-to-do peasant; but so slight an error hardly sticks in the throat after the gross ignorance of his contemporaries, and reviewers had some excuse when they praised the accuracy of his manners and costume. Tourneys, wandering knights, high-born ladies, castles, greenwood glades, woke in him a responsive thrill of glad romance. He may have read Malory, and he speaks as if Chaucer's poetry were not unknown to him; Ariosto must have come into his hands; and somewhere in the older romances he found the hint for the lighted, empty castle, whose radiance streams from the lights set about the coffin of the youthful bride of its lord, for the rock-built tower on the Elbe, where ferocious beasts guard every storey, and for the stately inter-change of sentiment which a reviewer stigmatized as the "weak, inefficient loves" of Richard de Clare and Geralda. These tastes, however, did not absorb more than a part of his lively imagination. He did not desire escape—to lose himself in the labyrinths of a fabulous mediaevalism. His books are hardly to be called "Gothick" at all. When he looked back through an arrow slit or a mullioned window at the landscape of the Middle Ages, he saw moving on its roads and in its halls a procession of modern follies in old-fashioned dress. He saw the Lady Ursulina, grandest and most dolorous of widowed women, satisfying her vanity by a parade of extravagantly complete mourning, which includes blowing her nose on a black handkerchief, dotting black gauze with black silk for amusement, and distributing broth to the poor in black porringers; he saw the shoulders of the Lady Isabella, which "as she lived with a correct mother and a maiden aunt . . . were immoderately down and back", and he watched the contortions of that courteous and inoffensive person, the Knight of the Porcupine, whose vain peculiarity it was "never to express either his opinions or his wishes, save only through the channel of a *hint*". The sojourners in the robbers' camp are marshalled into a parade of affectations; there is Sir Hubert, the modest Knight who strives to appear immodest, "attempting, with a countenance occasionally suffused with scarlet, to assume that cool and genuine impudence, which is unvarying, inveterate, incurable"; Sir Humphrey de Waverley who, in his anxiety not to seem affected, dances badly, deliberately mispronounces words, and on horseback "totters from side to side like a baker, his legs dangling after the manner of the meaner sort"; there is the Lady Hermundura, whose awkward vigour is more fitted to a dairymaid than a great lady; Sir Marmaduke who, knowing himself *damnably well built*, stands astride to exhibit the muscles of his thigh and "occasionally slaps his foot against the floor, and jerks his knee, until the calf of his leg truly quivers with the exertion"; and the unnamed traveller who "professes to have seen the world, and to know mankind, on the strength of having lain three nights at Antwerp, and bought a pair of breeches at Bruges", while he continually reminds his friends what a just taste in literature he has by such remarks as: "It is written in a blank leaf of my Amadis de Gaul—I have taken a memorandum of it in my Don Belianis—Did you see my Sir Bevis of Southampton anywhere?" Most of the time, in short, White is not looking into the past at all; he is borrowing its trappings to clothe the figures of his contemporaries.

His mild and sportive satire was not always aimed at the type. Apart from the parliamentary sketches, which were obvious and were recognized by contemporary reviewers, one suspects a good deal of individual portraiture which is not so readily traceable. Aix-la-Chapelle, where the husband-hunting of the lady who became Abbess of Heidelberg is finally defeated, is certainly Bath; and the Abbess herself, a tall dark woman with a disproportionately long waist, a prominent nose in an oval olive-skinned face, black hair, black, arching brows and large hazel eyes, has the look of a sketch from life. So have many other faces, often foolish and sometimes vicious, that glance at us for a moment out of helms or wimples, but do not stay long enough to take part in the story. Old Sir Reginald Fitzalan, whose head shakes with what White in softening sympathy calls the not ungraceful palsy of old age, who accompanies his gallant son to the jousts and discourses of the past with a venerable garrulity, is perhaps Lord Camden; the evidence in the book is insufficient in itself, but Camden had championed public rights in England and liberal treatment of Ireland, he had a son, a later Lord Lieutenant of Ireland, who was then coming to the fore, he was closely connected with Bath where White had relations, and to him was addressed White's last book, so that he may well have arranged for him this brief and sympathetic appearance in the masquerade. The three Directors of Moralities point to Garrick, Foote and, perhaps, Colman— the Abbot is speaking of his youth—and Friar Matthew, who aims at perfect propriety of speech and entreats yet resents criticism, is reminiscent of Cumberland; but who is the Countess of Zurellenburg, noted for early rising, with her four fair, well-educated daughters, who excel in the new French dances? Slight as these figures are, they have the air of something individual and observed. More substantial is the Lord Bishop of Bamberg in *Cœur-de-Lion*. This able and latitudinarian prelate, a builder and patron of art, a strict disciplinarian in his bishopric, where he compels the clergy to reside on their cures without feeling himself bound to set them an example, wisely charitable to the poor, scandalizing the pious by his flippant behaviour in society, his Sunday evening music meetings and the little reverence he seems to pay to Christianity, is almost certainly Frederick Augustus Hervey, Bishop of Derry and Earl of Bristol, patron of Ann Yearsley and many others. He makes an impressive appearance in the romance, travelling about the Continent in opulent state with his train of servants and sumpter-waggons. "I love a little luxury, I vow the God", is his unperturbed remark to the King, and that monarch is divided between disapproval and admiration of the "mixture of profaneness and attention to the interests of religion, of solidity and levity" in this well-developed eighteenth-century personality. Over his royalties White had to be more careful. The four young princes in *John of Gaunt* gave him a chance that was too good to take. There is therefore nothing of the Prince of Wales in the idealized Black Prince, unless we are to find ironical intention in his dignity among friends, his rigid discretion in the choice of them and his noble renunciation of the Lady Ermenilda. The Duke of York recalls George III's second son only by his "unlimited attachment" to his elder brother and perhaps by his indolence, for this was the Carlton House stage of Frederick's life. The suggestions of the future William III are a little stronger in the ambitious, restless, generous and self-sufficient Duke of Gloucester; but these are not allusions that can be pressed; the four princes-errant are mostly figures of romance.

The fun of the masquerade is carried into small corners of the books. It is the fun of wearing antique costume without changing one's modern mind, and of finding mediaeval equivalents for familiar habits of thought and action. Hermits' cells were presumably property, and a disgusted fugitive from the world may therefore reasonably be supposed to purchase a cave from the executors of a deceased recluse and take over his furniture at a fair valuation. What the furniture consisted of we hear from the Lady Philippina de Clairvaux who is concealing herself in the disguise of a hermit from a troublesome husband, and has been provided by her maid's uncle, who is in the profession, with a cave, beards for both ladies, proper attire, a little bed, a table, two benches, some porringers, two kittens, a crutch, a poker and a crucifix. No doubt armourers, as well as tailors, had difficulty in getting in their money and misspent their time, waiting in base courts and barbicans for creditors who presently pranced over the drawbridge and dismissed them with a condescending nod and a "So, Timothy!" Heiresses who in the eighteenth century thrilled to an embroidered waistcoat might be caught in the twelfth by an adventurer in tastefully inlaid armour with false calves in his greaves and a glorious red beard; and the Lady Barbarina's romances are smuggled in to her, like Lydia Languish's, by her maid, though the source of corruption is not in this case a circulating library but a Benedictine of a neighbouring monastery. Books provide a charming opportunity for blending the two strains. When Strongbow visits the wounded Earl of Northumberland, he finds his squire reading aloud to him *Amadis of Gaul*. Strongbow recommends *Bevis of Hampton*, while admitting that the style is not so affecting and sublime as that of *Amadis*. Northumberland is anxious to read the history of *Charlemagne*, but the only manuscript is at Glastonbury, and the monks refuse to lend it, even though Northumberland has offered to pledge the Barony of Warkworth in return. So the two gentlemen develop their literary tastes in the face of the most picturesque difficulties.

It is doubtful whether all this pleasantly incongruous material could be fused together into a harmonious narrative; it is certain that White did not try to do it. His talent was purely episodic; he could never sustain a theme or a mood. Taking the obvious plan of the wandering knight, he led his hero in and out of detached adventures and suffered him to meet other travellers, who exchange histories with him. The tone is never the same for a dozen pages together, except in the oratorical set pieces, where the formal diction, inflated slightly beyond the degree of eloquence, bathes the scene in a steady light of mingled admiration and amusement. Elsewhere the gathering suggestions of romance are broken by boyish shouts of mirth, while sometimes across the gaiety tolls the passing bell. He is continually oversetting his romantic figures and standing them up again. The attitude of the heroic fighter will suddenly become contorted with a fabulous extravagance, congenial to the Celtic imagination, but in this case probably imitated from Ariosto. Thus Strongbow, in his encounter with the robbers, pins one malefactor immoveably to the trunk of a tree with his lance and whips off the head of another with such force that, "after spinning through the air for some moments, [it] descended at a distance from the scene of strife, and was lost amidst the weeds and brambles of the forest". The story of the assault on the castle of Dinas Bran begins in the best Arthurian way, with the appearance at Llewellyn's court of a melancholy dame in sable apparel and Strongbow's vow never to sleep in a bed, eat from a tablecloth, comb his beard or put off his armour until he has redressed her injuries, but it ends with the discovery of the caitiff chieftain of the stronghold under an inverted basket in the corner of the great kitchen. Sometimes the modulation is the other way, from jest to earnest, and the loss of the fair Geralda and the death of the Black Prince draw notes of sad emotion from this odd jester. It is these notes, together with his touches of woodland beauty and the mischievous grace of his girls, that check the otherwise obvious comparison with the *Ingoldsby Legends*.

In his first novel, *Strongbow*, there is a larger measure of the romantic and elegiac than in the two that followed. Here he bestowed his material within a double frame and approached his scene with three measured strides. The book begins in the Gothic mood with a picturesque and orthodox description of Chepstow Castle, and is already set back fifty years in time. An old woman leads the traveller through dark vaults, unsafe stair-cases, roofless halls, cheerless kitchens, a chapel no longer holy;—bade me peep through spike-holes, climb battlements, descend through winding passages, squeeze through narrow wickets;—craved my assistance to raise bars, loosen bolts, unlock doors, all which appeared neither rotten nor sound, but in that sort of stationary condition, which tells one that time has been weary of afflicting them.

This sentimental and antiquarian rambling was a recognized vacation exercise of the later eighteenth century; Walpole had indulged in it twenty-five years before, and Mrs Radcliffe, beginning in this very year of 1789, was to make it a full-time occupation. But this angle of vision does not satisfy White. He takes another step backwards by means of a manuscript, the work of a prisoner in the Castle during the reign of Charles I. The style begins to show touches of archaic state-liness, and the writer begins to mock himself in his reverie. The prisoner has met on the battlements the ghost of Richard de Clare, called Strongbow, Earl of Pembroke and conqueror of Leinster, and has heard in a series of nocturnal interviews the story of his life. White is not serious about his ghost, though he is about some of the things he has to tell. He considers the situation practically. Strongbow, of course, speaks Norman-French, but luckily the prisoner has studied law. Schooled in noble reserve, he finds some difficulty in recounting his own exploits, but points out that as he is confined to verbal narration he cannot imitate the modesty of Cæsar and refer to himself in the third person. On the other hand, he defends himself for not using the obligatory hollow tone in which the spirits of the departed address the living; it is mere affectation, he declares, intended to give an air of consequence to what they say. White drenches his spectre with a midnight shower, but lays occasional grave words on his sententious tongue, as is his freakish way; Strongbow is laughing-stock one minute and oracle the next. We enter the book, then, through such an ivy-covered arch

as frames the distance in many a contemporary print. Beyond
the arch are persons and scenes which we are to behold under
a threefold aspect. There is first the historical material proper,
the picture of unfamiliar social conditions, the tournaments,
the Irish women in their saffron smocks and forehead cloths,
the Earl of Salisbury's household where Strongbow is brought
up in the usages of chivalry—nothing substantial or picturesque enough to keep White's name alive after *Waverley*
appeared, but enough to please critics at this early stage of
the historical novel. Secondly, there is common human
nature, mostly in farcical relations, and speaking, in spite of
hauberks and morions, with the inflections of the eighteenth
century. Lastly there is the masquerade, the fun of deliberate
incongruity, personal identifications and "dressing-up". The
brevity of the nocturnal interviews with the ghost, like that of
John of Gaunt's visits to Mortimer's sick-bed, which con-
stitute the structual device of *John of Gaunt*, acknowledges the
heterogeneity and disconnection of the materials; and the
parting salutes of both visitors are apt to contain the flicker
of a wink. In these pocket instalments we range from Geralda's
austerely guarded avowal of noble affection to a contemptuous
view of Wexford with its ruinous fortifications, its ground
littered with drunken shapes after a holiday and "bestrewn
with fragments of provisions, embers of peat, oystershells,
fish-bones, wooden platters"; from Strongbow receiving at
the Countess of Salisbury's hands his ancestor's sword,
Gridalbin, to Strongbow opposing jobbery in Ireland. The
first job, we are told, was a monopoly for providing Dublin
with oysters and rabbits on a five-year contract, rashly
bestowed by Strongbow on his ill-conditioned squire Otho,
but it opened the door to such flagrant abuses that he was
forced to resume his grants; and here the earl's features settle
into a momentary likeness to those of Lord Temple who, as
Lord Lieutenant in 1782-3 and again when *Strongbow* was
published, had endeavoured to suppress petty fraud among the

minor officials of the state. "By God's blessing, I made them honest in spite of their teeth," growls the spectre, a remark his secretary relegates to a footnote, as being "somewhat less dignified than the rest of his discourse".

In his second romance White developed his method a little further and tilted his medley more persistently towards mirth. Here and in *Cœur-de-Lion* he traces in outline anecdotes that would work up excellently into fantastic farce. In *John of Gaunt* there is the episode of the monster in the Isle of Man, who delights in taking captive the high-born and fastidious and subjecting them to a course of menial labour, "to season them with that philosophy which is the offspring of woe". There the scandalized Sir Allen Mac Fergus sees the King of Kerry gutting a turkey, the Abbot of St Alban's wheeling out manure and his own princess of the Orkneys in a deplorable perspiration, wringing a pair of sheets. This gay castigation of rank is matched in *Cœur-de-Lion* by the story of the Baron of Ramillies who gets a living out of his impoverished noble blood by staying in a centre of bourgeois snobbery and selling his salutes according to a regular tariff. White sets out the terms of his contract with the widow of a tax collector, who is a social climber. In return for a subsidy of a hundred florins a month, runs the document, "you, the Lord Baron of Ramillies, are to allow her full liberty of accosting you in public places, of nodding to you, smiling at you, and even tapping you on the shoulder:...for extraordinary acts of familiarity, such as whispering you, tittering with you, or talking to you for a long time, an extraordinary consideration will be expected: that is to say, a sum of money not less than forty florins." This contract serves as a model for others, and the ambitious wives of Ratisbon cut down their housekeeping expenses and economize on their children's education to pay the Baron's stipend. It is characteristic of White that the hero of this picaresque episode is not lost to grace; he is conscious of unknightly behaviour and troubled at the domestic disorder

he occasions. "I became as it were a pestilence," he sighs with
one of those odd, fleeting hints of sentiment that everywhere
accompany the farce. The situation is terminated by a vivid
explosion at a fashionable christening, where two of his pay
mistresses jostle at his elbow for attention, break out into
rivalry, and substantiate their claims with the unanswerable
revelation: "I have paid my money for it!" "And I too,
madam!"

There is a great deal of varied material in the three books,
the scattered notions of a whimsical and flighty rather than
a truly inventive mind. There are compressed picaresque
narratives that glance like candle beams over mediaeval
Europe, picking out here the Flemish weavers and the
wreckers on the Frisian coast, there the Crusades, the Jewish
persecutions and the slaves in the Moorish Kingdom of
Granada. There are also Lucianic adventures, a visit to the
island of Ferro, where Harpocrates is worshipped and no loud
sound shivers the silence; an abduction to an underground
city in Muscovy, inhabited by a remnant of fire worshippers;
and a bold Arctic expedition, on which the explorers, armed
with solidified soup and cooking stoves, discover a temperate
sea about the Pole and scrupulously record the fauna of the
district. There are inset poems, including a versification in
the style of Cowley of selected passages from the Psalms; and
there are pleasant glimpses of landscape, such as the autumnal
lake where from the Lady Ursulina's black boat her retainers
fish for the box containing the narrative of the "super-
eminently villainous" hermit Voltello, or the forest glades
through which the escaping nuns and novices scud on their
ponies, leaving a ponderous lady abbess lamenting under an
oak tree. Mountains raised in White the full romantic
response; they elevated and purified his mind; and the couplets
in which he celebrates their power have some poetry in them.

Both his burlesque and his solemnity received the gloss of
an artificially stately style. It is the sort of style that might

have been developed in an eighteenth-century student by the practice of translation. In poetry he charged his quatrains with words like "querimonious" and "praeterfluent", and in prose he called a sword a refulgent falchion and made one of his characters remark of the enemy's sentries: "Inebriety will encroach upon their accustomed vigilance." But he also shook a reviewer by speaking of a "snotty-looking baron", and occasionally suffered his young ladies to slide into the colloquial. "I wish he were come," wails the Lady Matilda, benighted in the woods without her usher; "for, my dear, it waxes late and forests are dangerous places. Full of Hermits." He liked an assemblage of strong and sounding adjectives, and he liked balanced and antithetical sentences, weighted with appositional phrases. Even the ravished and rescued damsel must not be syntactically disarrayed. "That I have not been bereft of my honour, perhaps too of my life, I bless the eternal saints, and glorify the Queen of Heaven," says the stately Geralda; "that Earl Strongbow was the instrument of my safety, is an additional source of undissembled satisfaction." There is a good deal of the mock-heroic about this style, but it is also the kind of language that came naturally to White in his serious moments. It is never dead; its exuberant outlines have been shaped to gratify the author's taste; and occasionally they quiver with amusement, with some slightly unexpected collocation of words, not remarkable in themselves but remarkable in so ceremonious a context. Thus we learn of a lady's "rocky insensitiveness" and hear a young man describe how he went "strenuously to church". These are the dimples and eddies in the majestic stream of his eloquence.

Cœur-de-Lion was White's last novel. The critics, in spite of some disquietude at this odd caricature of the "Dignity of Heroism" and a general misgiving about the educational and literary status of the historical novel, had been on the whole complimentary. *Cœur-de-Lion* had broken down the defences of even the austere *Monthly* reviewer, and he admitted to reading it, shaking his sides and his head at the same time. I have found no other allusions to the three books or to their fortune with the public. White himself, in the first pages of *Cœur-de-Lion*, draws up a light-handed account of the opinions of mantua-makers, boarding-schools, viscountesses and milliners, from which we learn that he has been criticized for his language and the slightness of his love interest, and that the terms of chivalry, comprehensible enough to high-born ladies who had read Ariosto, were a stumbling-block to the milliners. Obviously little importance is to be attached to these remarks, but even so he makes up his claims on popularity with some confidence. Next year he returned to translation. His versions both of Mirabeau's speeches and of St Étienne's history are informed by a sober approval of the Revolution, though he is careful to make it very clear that England stands in no need of so drastic a medicine. Certain minor rectifications, including a more equal distribution of the ecclesiastical preferment—a subject on which the outlaw, Raymond of the Bushy Beard, had had unexpectedly strong opinions—are all that is required. In Mirabeau White sees once more his ideal, the orator-statesman, harnessing the emotions of his hearers in the service of justice and patriotism. "Bravo!" he exclaims in a footnote; and again: "I experience the highest pleasure in transfusing the spirit of this patriot out of his language into mine. Let me cry, almost in the words of Corregio, 'Anch' Io sono oratore'." It all sounds vigorous and healthy enough, and we learn from the *Critical Review* that he had other schemes for translation in hand. But at this point he disappears from our view, and the next record of him is contained in the *European Magazine* for April 1799.

In the course of the last month was found dead in his bed at the Carpenter's Arms, a public house in the parish of Wick, Gloucestershire, about 6 miles from Bath, James White, Esq., a gentleman well-known in the literary world.

The obituary notice follows. He was known, we are told, as an admirable scholar, but for the last four or five years his conduct had been marked by great wildness and eccentricity. "He had conceived an ardent affection for a certain young lady, who, he supposed, was as warmly attached to him; but (as he imagined) some plot had been contrived to wean his regard and to frustrate all his future prospects in life." These are the old imaginations, focused on a more painful loss and strengthened by the failure of some application for patronage which he had made. In *Strongbow* he had compared the man pursued by misfortune to "a bullrush growing in the midst of a stream, and maintaining a perpetual struggle against the current, that with unceasing opposition now presses down its head, now suffers it to rise some small degree, now sinks it utterly beneath the wave". The image well conveys his unhappiness.

"The winters of 1797 and 1798", continues the *European Magazine*, "he passed in the neighbourhood of Bath; and many of our readers may often have noticed in the pump-room, the streets or the vicinity of the city, a thin, pale, emaciated man (between thirty and forty) with a wild yet penetrating look, dressed in a light coat of Bath coating. His means of subsistence were very scanty; and he obliged the cravings of nature to keep within their limits. He has been known to have debarred himself of animal food for months, and to have given life a bare subsistence by a biscuit, a piece of bread, or a cold potatoe and a glass of water. Unable to pay his lodgings and too proud to ask relief, he would many nights wander about the fields, or seek repose beneath a hay-stack, almost exhausted. He once took refuge in an inn in Bath, where his extraordinary conduct, and his refusing every sustenance, alarmed the mistress, and impelled her to apply to the magistrates, who humanely ordered him to be put under the care of a parish-officer. Instead of appreciating these precautionary means as he ought to have done, he, in letters to some persons in the city complained of "the undue interference of magisterial authority and this unconstitutional infringement of the liberty of the subject".

The "Dignity of Heroism" was as oddly caricatured in his actions as it had been by his pen.

He remained keenly interested in politics. We hear of certain *Letters to Lord Camden on the State of Ireland*, written in one of the intervals when his mind was more composed, and much admired for "the elegance and strength of his language, the shrewdness of his remarks, and the perspicacity of his arguments". The *European Magazine* states clearly that they were published but gives no date, and I have not been able to trace them. At last a small subscription was raised privately for his relief and he was with difficulty prevailed on to accept it as a loan. At about this time, but probably after the money was exhausted, he left Bath for Wick, a village six miles to the north on the Bristol road. He was a walker, and the romantic, watered valley, overhung by the rocks which Gainsborough drew, with its Roman camp and "Druidical" stones, must have been already familiar to him. His proceedings there were ascertained in detail by the *Monthly Magazine*.

On the 11th of March he went to Wick, and there remained that night; after breakfast the next day he went to Bath, and returned again in the evening. Wednesday being an unpleasant day, he remained indoors, amusing himself with such publications as the house afforded. On Friday night he ordered some tea and retired to bed about nine. Not arising at his usual hour, the mistress of the house sent up to him, when he complained of a slight indisposition, and passed the whole day in his bed, refusing to take the least nutriment. On the evening of the following day he expired.

A coroner's inquest was called, and its finding may be reflected in the following entry in the register of the Church of St James, Abson:

1799. James White, Esq: (he ended his existence by Famine —supposed to be insane) his name not learnt for sometime. March 15th.

The date, if the *Monthly Magazine* is right, should be 18 March.

We may let that elegiac pen conclude the obituary of the poor clerk.

One shilling and two sixpences was all the pecuniary store he had; and as he died amongst strangers, he was buried at the expense of a person to whom he was utterly unknown; and though an admirable scholar, possessed of most brilliant parts, and generally admired for the elegance and strength of his language, he now lies buried in Abson Churchyard, without a stone or letter to mark the place of his interment.

He had enjoyed some reputation, both at home and abroad. *Strongbow* was put into French, and there was a German translation of that and of *John of Gaunt*. He cannot be considered as one of the romantic misfits of the eighteenth century; his age suited him; his jolly piping was heard even in that noisy time and half-reluctant critics danced to it. A curious ear may discern the rift in the instrument, but it would be a fault in proportion to let such slight performances bear a burden of tragic significance; *The Yeomen of the Guard* is not a tragedy because at the end Jack Point staggers out and dies. The books are best taken for what they are, the pastime of a scholar and a wit, not occasioning any change in the English novel—for the future was with the heavier and far less civilized fare of Sophia Lee, Ann Radcliffe and the Gothic romance—but standing modestly in the company of those that have combined burlesque and beauty, enthusiasm and laughter. White is distinguished from Barham by the absence of the macabre note in him and the presence of moments of idyllic and mischievous grace; and one would not cow the shade of a writer who cries aloud for illustration by Mr George Morrow by adducing greater names. He is nearest in tone to the far sturdier, more intellectual and humanly substantial Peacock. They had many tastes in common, for Welsh mountains and antiquities, for farce and poetry, for eloquent, sustained argument, for plump, worldly churchmen and spirited girls, and for the picturesque emphasis that is laid on human folly by dressing it up in the clothes of long ago. It goes without saying that all this material is far slighter in White and more casually arranged, and that the exquisitely poignant and ludicrous allegory of Seithenyn's embankment is as much beyond his simple burlesque as the poetry of its breaking is beyond the careful stiffness of his eloquence. Nevertheless, White is a finger-post to Peacock, and it is very disappointing that there is no evidence that he ever lifted his eyes to it or followed its slender digit.

MARY HAYS, PHILOSOPHESS

∧∧∧∧∧∧∧∧∧∧∧∧

O F all the small writers whom this book commemorates, Mary Hays is the least likely to be quite forgotten. This is not because of the quality of her literary work, which is, with the exception of *The Scotch Parents*, the worst we have handled, since she rejected the discipline of eighteenth-century taste and acquired no other; but because she passed many years of her life on the edge of a circle that is still intrinsically interesting to us. She was the occasion of characteristic utterances by Lamb, Southey and Coleridge, and is to be found modestly posted in explanatory footnotes to their correspondence. She knew Mary Wollstonecraft, and was counted by the *Anti-Jacobin* among those "philosophesses" who blasphemously controverted the real nature of woman in their vindication of her political and economic rights; and she deposited a great deal of confidence in the cool bosom of William Godwin. Her novels, *The Memoirs of Emma Courtney* and *The Victim of Prejudice*, are occasionally cited as documents in the history of feminism; and recently a collateral descendant, Miss A. F. Wedd, has published a selection from the love-letters of her girlhood, followed by the letters addressed to her in middle life by Mrs Eliza Fenwick, with an introduction based on family papers.[1] What follows is little more than a

[1] *The Love-Letters of Mary Hays* and *The Fate of the Fenwicks* (Methuen). For permission to quote from these books I am indebted to the author and the publishers.

leisurely reconsideration of all this material, paying less attention to her not very important contacts with the romantic poets
than to her self-portrait in *Emma Courtney*, that astonishing
blend of complacence and a white sheet.

It is pleasant that a book which began with Elizabeth
Griffith should end with Mary Hays. They were born within
about thirty years of each other, but the cleft between their
two generations was more than usually deep, and the difference
in temperament between them is reinforced by differences in
modes of thought and expression. Mrs Griffith had asserted
that the only philosophy a woman ought to have was resignation. Miss Hays was strenuously philosophical and not at all
resigned. She was a Godwinite, measuring right and wrong
by the scale of social utility. She accepted the mechanical
theory of the Universe and managed to harmonize it with
Christianity. Her mouth was full of catchwords and quotations, and she did, with painful labour and some sophistication,
seek to understand what happened to her in the light of these
beliefs; but in the contortions with which she accepted her
fate resignation was the last posture she tried. Hers is the
clamour of constant outrage. A distempered civilization has
wronged her; she has a case to bring against the prejudices of
society; and the brawling, repetitive egoism with which she
brings it contrasts strongly with Mrs Griffith's plaintive
delicacy. Confession was at once a need of her nature and her
strongest weapon of offence. Her scientific interest in her own
case quelled shamefastness as it must have quenched her sense
of humour and her fear of ridicule; moreover the consequences
of injustice must be exhibited in order that justice may be done.
In her lifetime her friends bore the brunt of her vehement
and undesired candour; and now she has found another ear.

"You never wrote . . . an all-of-the-wrong-side sloping hand,
like Miss Hayes" (*sic*), says Lamb in a letter to George Dyer.
The tiny fact, thrown out in a soothing, mirthful expostulation
with the ruffled Dyer, who had been pricked by an allusion to

his hieroglyphics, rejoices the heart as that of Edmund Gosse was rejoiced when he found it recorded that Joseph Warton read the Communion Service in a remarkably awful manner. Its appropriateness is perfect. Her reaction from the ethics of womanhood as the eighteenth century had understood them, from reserve, complaisance and submission, had indeed sent Miss Hays sloping all of the wrong side. Her chance of establishing herself in an upright position, never very good in one of her temperament, was destroyed when the death of her first lover and her repeated failures to attract another left her deepest needs unsatisfied; and in her quest for fulfilment she was led into acts of aggression that are a comic parody on the sexual honesty which her friends, the philosophers, declared to be more modest than concealment. None the less, she remained courageous, generous and determined to profit by her experiences. She looked forward to the emancipation of womanhood and the regeneration of society, and she looked steadily forward, unlike many of her friends, to a life beyond the grave. She was a grotesque, but, in the eighteenth-century meaning of the word, a respectable one.

Mary Hays was one of a family of sisters, and when she met John Eccles she was living with her widowed mother in Gainsford Street, Southwark. John Eccles lodged so near that, as their romance developed, they could communicate by signs from window to window; a book laid against hers meant that she was alone and could be visited, while his drawn curtain in the early morning, when she is already up and penning her daily letter, brings down on him an arch rebuke. They had met at chapel; both were liberal dissenters with a taste for a good sermon, but Eccles soon makes it clear that those provided at their place of worship would not ensure his attendance if it were not for the presence of Mary. She was then about nineteen, small—her short legs were to provide material for caricature—with few personal charms, as she sadly admitted in hope of contradiction, impulsive, enthusiastic, intermittently prudish, and very much occupied with her own sensibility. To Eccles she appeared "a little girl with dark hair and features soft as the peaceful messengers of heaven", and he was very soon assuring her—assuring and reassuring became his daily portion—that compared with her not even Petrarch's Laura would attract a moment's attention from him. Their letters begin early in 1779, when she was about nineteen, and are soon charged with all the emotions of interrupted affection. John Eccles was without immediate prospects; his home was at Fordingbridge in Hampshire, where he had worked in his father's business, but his endeavours to enlarge and improve it had been checked by paternal disapproval, and he was now in London, lending some kind of unpaid or slightly paid assistance in a friend's office, with a good deal of time on his hands. Mr Eccles senior, when his son made known to him the state of his affections, refused to take the matter seriously, and Mrs Hays had to intervene to separate the lovers. There were at least two parting scenes, rich in emotion. Mary abstained from food for twenty-four hours and relinquished her night's rest in order to be in a fit state to bid John Eccles farewell; her apologetic lover found the flesh too weak to fulfil his part of the vigil; but he made amends by a description of his face in the morning. "I am now looking in the glass," he wrote to the exigent and unhappy girl over the way, "and really I pity myself. I am observing the force of passion; in what strong colours it lives in every feature; how visible the marks of love and disappointment sit there." They met and parted, but not for long. Mary was tenacious and Eccles was unemployed, and both were certainly in love. A clandestine daily correspondence began, of enormous bulk and inevitably monotonous quality, and presently there were clandestine excursions too, to Vauxhall and further afield to Greenwich. Sister Betsy aided and abetted, and the indulgent Mrs Hays, we must believe, turned a blind eye. No doubt even then Mary was ill to cross.

There is little intellectual substance in the letters and no
literary grace. Yet the lovers plainly feel themselves to be
cultivated people; they enjoyed mediocre sentimental poetry;
Eccles called himself Mary's "literary beau" and was prepared to argue on behalf of the immortality of the soul from
the evidence of dreams, while Mary already shows a taste for
disputation. She meant to be a good girl and had to discuss
the why and how. Their letters, then, show none of the
reflective range of Henry and Frances, but they convey
character, of an immature kind, with equal vigour though less
pleasurably. Mary was, as Miss Wedd has observed, at once
daring and prim; she committed herself to Eccles's keeping on
country excursions, but at the least lover-like demonstration
complained that he treated her with "extreme freedom" and
anxiously probed his opinion of her delicacy. She was very
much agitated over her delicacy and discussed it a good deal.
She accepted it, as all educated girls of her generation did, as
one of her most important obligations, for without delicacy
what becomes of the civilizing function of women? But she
was also sure of the importance of candour and sincerity.
Delicacy probably meant restraint, but it could not mean
concealment. Her inability to conceal, or to consider the
sensibilities of others when her own were in full play, was a
permanent trait of her character, and in later years transformed
her conception of delicacy into a highly aggressive virtue; but
she never ceased to use the word. At present, however, she
had many scruples about the exact balance of the two qualities,
and Eccles had often to compose them. He told her, in
heartfelt compliment, that she had invariably been honest;
she had never played the artful with him; he would "venture
to oppose *decent* freedom against an *affected* reserve: the former
is one of the loveliest parts of your character, 'tis where I see
you with the most affectionate sensations." Decent freedom,
however, might not perhaps include embraces. "I cannot
help thinking I was too passive last night (you know what I

mean)," writes Mary with misgiving; "I cannot reconcile my conduct to those strict rules of delicacy which I had determined ever to adhere to." Delicacy and a certain kittenish playfulness defeated candour when it came to putting a name to the sensations which absorbed her. She availed herself of asterisks or a simple cipher and reminds him in melting quotation that "May is the month of L 452!"

Eccles did not have an altogether easy time. He had to write every day, and he had to assure his Maria (sometimes Polly, but more often the statelier syllables) not only that he wanted to write, but that he had plenty to write about and would have plenty, however long the correspondence lasted. He had to digest, in a single missive from his lady, the most irritating suspicions and the most plaintive appeals for pity on behalf of "your poor little girl", who "has been early initiated to sufferings", and he was goaded into writing indignant letters which he sometimes tore up next day, and sometimes sent as a warning, accompanied by a remorseful postscript. She feared his displeasure with an excessive timidity and provoked it by her restless qualms. "Am I not a little monopolizing girl to confine you in this manner?" she writes, seeking to disarm censure by the implied flattery. "But you must forgive me, for as Mrs Digby says: 'I cannot bear a rival in love or friendship.'" John forgave her. "All things considered, I think I am a good kind of young man," he writes with meek humour. Once he was driven beyond his patience, and for some days tried to affect indifference to his little girl; but it was a vain expedient and most uncomfortable, for: "Whilst I looked at her with a countenance dégagée, the warmest perplexities reigned within." Once or twice, too, he wrote her a manly and reasonable protest against their "petty tumults", and presently he feels able to congratulate her on having overcome them. Their prospects also had brightened. Mary's tenacity had at last forced the family into action. One of her brothers-in-law had been pressed into

service; acceptable proposals, including some sort of partner-
ship for the young man, had been made to Mr Eccles senior,
and by July 1780 Mary Hays and John Eccles were publicly
engaged. What followed is quickly told. Eccles, whose health
had given Mary cause for anxiety for some weeks, grew rapidly
worse. It was thought that his native air might check the
decline, and he prepared to leave London. Before he left,
Mary went to his lodgings and sat by his bed. She never saw
him again, nor did he even reach Fordingbridge. He died at
Salisbury, in the house of a relation, in his last wanderings
often calling on the name of "his dear Miss Polly Hays", and
attempting to sing or repeat a line or two of the hymns they
had sung together in Chapel.

Mary received the news with the full violence of her nature.

Wild, distracted, and outrageous, I accused Providence, and my
Creator! I stamped on the earth in an agony of despair, and made
the house echo with my cries; at last my spirits were exhausted, and
I sunk into insensibility and stupidity: for three days refused all
refreshment—I shed no tears—my senses were confused—my head
seemed disordered—I talked calmly but very incoherently—my
eyes were fixed, and I scarcely changed my position.

Her friends were very naturally alarmed. Her mother permitted her to put on mourning for her lover, and she vowed
never to quit it. The Eccleses invited her to Fordingbridge,
and, while considering whether the visit would make her feel
better or worse, and whether she wanted to feel better or
worse, she began an impassioned correspondence with the
eldest Miss Eccles. She was always fiercely competitive in
her griefs, and was now concerned to prove that her loss was
far greater than a sister's could be. "He was all I saw in the
creation," she wrote. "... May this heart cease to beat should
it ever be capable of feeling emotions of tenderness for any
other than its first, and only love." She went to Fordingbridge
in the autumn and vowed eternal fidelity to Eccles, kneeling
on his grave. She was then twenty, and before a month is over,

with that saving honesty that always struggles out from beneath
her emotionalism, she is admitting that she has experienced
some soothing moments, blended perceptions of scenery,
conscious innocence and pride in the quality of her own tenderness. The Eccles family worked hard to entertain her. We
hear of an excursion to the New Forest, to drink tea in a
keeper's lodge and return by moonlight, and of discussions
with Mr Eccles, in which the relative merits of Charles I and
Cromwell were debated, and his Arminian principles wrestled
politely with his young guest's Unitarianism. Mary liked
Hampshire.

"The country abounds with murmuring brooks and purling
streams, which you know are objects I am partial to," she wrote
to her mother, adding: "I am become quite a drinker of their ale,
which I think very fine. In mentioning my amusements I forgot
to tell you, that I have bought a little rabbit, which I have rendered
quite tame; it eats out of my hands and sleeps in my chamber,
in a basket of tow—he is now sitting by my side, munching some
bran.—But how trifling is all this! how foreign to my heart! a heart
labouring under mixed pain, and the deepest regrets! struggling
with sorrow that dissolves it in tenderness and anguish."

Her youthful vitality was reasserting itself, but the blow had
been heavy. On the anniversary of her loss she is still wearing
mourning and hoping for death. Devotion seemed her only
refuge; she had loved John Eccles idolatrously, and he had
been taken from her.

At this point we lose sight of the girl Mary Hays. When she
reappears some eleven years later, it is as Eusebia, friend of
philosophers, authoress of a pamphlet on public worship,
"a disciple of truth", according to her own description, "and
a contemner of the artificial forms which have served but to
corrupt and enslave society". Eccles was not forgotten, but
she no longer wore sables for him; indeed, if we may trust the
caricature of her in Miss Elizabeth Hamilton's *Memoirs of
Modern Philosophers*, her dress was eccentric and gaudy. The

wig, which too precariously crowned Miss Bridgetina
Botherim, cannot with certainty be brought home to Mary
Hays, but when the ungentlemanly *English Review* called her
"the baldest disciple of Mrs Wollstonecraft", there was
perhaps more than literary criticism to barb the taunt. She
was aware that she was out of the ordinary, and felt that her
eccentricities were the natural and not unsympathetic result
of her experiences. In her *Letters and Essays, Moral and Miscellaneous* (1793), she tells with altered circumstances the story
of her own frustrated love. The heroine, like Mary, abandons
herself to grief, till, shocked to perceive herself on the brink
of hypochondria, she rallies her forces for a deliberate recovery.
The impressions of her tragedy "became at length the remem-
brance of remembrances, and if they betrayed her into some
little whimsicality of character, the deviations were such as
to the humane and philosophic eye, tracing back effects to
causes, rendered her more dear and interesting". Her pen
played a part in her convalescence, dimly seen in the scarcity
of record. The love-letters, preserved, as Miss Wedd describes
them, in a careful and beautiful transcription by Mary's friend,
Mrs Collier, were edited by Mary herself with an introduction
and notes. She embarked upon but failed to finish a tale,
Edwin, which was to enshrine Eccles as its hero. We hear also
of a criticism of the moral tendency of *Werther*, which was sent
by a friend to the *Universal Magazine* and afterwards reprinted
in the second edition of the English translation. But it was
by way of her religious interests that Miss Hays climbed on
to a wider stage. At some point the devotionalism that
assuaged her grief for John Eccles must have stiffened into a
course of solid reading. She belonged to a reasoning, intellectual sect and liked the forms of argument. When therefore
the scholar and controversialist Gilbert Wakefield, whose
religious views harmonized in general with her own, proposed
his opinion that public devotions are in some sort a corruption
of the act of worship, which should be solitary, inward and

contemplative, Mary, though with some showy trepidation in her preface and conclusion, was able to write him a sensible rejoinder. Her little pamphlet, *Cursory Remarks on an Enquiry into the Expediency and Propriety of Public or Social Worship* (1792), was well received by her dissenting friends and by the press. The *English Review* amiably referred to it as an "elegant and polite little performance". Ministers and prominent laymen wrote to her, and the indulgent circle of friends and relations, which all records invite us to presume, was widened to include men of some public importance. The dissenting background— in particular the Unitarian background—is constant through-out her life. She knew the family of the Reverend Robert Robinson, and George Dyer, that absent-minded scholar, who had been tutor there, arranged a tea party for her to meet Dr Priestley. The Reverend Hugh Worthington of Salter's Hall encouraged her to write her *Letters and Essays,* and Dr Disney of Essex Street Chapel obligingly preached some sermons that she wrote. A long and polite letter came from Cambridge from a recent convert to Unitarianism, the mathematician and Hebrew scholar, William Frend, whose propagation of his new opinions had already cost him his tutorship at Jesus College, and was in a year's time to bring on him a prosecution in the Vice-Chancellor's Court and a sentence of banishment from the University. They had not then met, but, complimenting her on her "sentiments un-sophisticated by scholastick learning", he expressed the wish that they might one day discuss their common faith together. Meanwhile George Dyer had brought her Mary Wollstone-craft's *Vindication of the Rights of Women,* and, strongly stimu-lated by a manifesto which endeavoured, in her own words, to "restore degraded woman to the glory of rationality, and to a fitness for immortality", she wrote to the author and presently made her acquaintance at the house of Johnson the publisher. A cool and friendly criticism of the *Cursory Remarks,* touching with a firm finger its passages of egoism, remains to prove the shrewdness and kindliness of the greater Mary. Both these last names are of great importance in the life of Miss Hays; from Mary Wollstonecraft she learnt that feminism which, in her own crude version, became her constant creed, and in William Frend she thought she saw a successor to John Eccles.

The painful affair with William Frend—if that may be called an affair where all the activity is on one side while the other remains distressed and repellent—took place before Mary Hays begins to move across the pages of Lamb and Southey. She had already, however, enrolled herself among the philosophers, the circle of literary thinkers in close sympathy with the French Revolution, whose social theories were given their most challenging and unmitigated expression in Godwin's *Political Justice*. This small circle overlapped the larger one of the liberal dissenters and entry into it must have been easy enough, especially as she could rely on the good offices of George Dyer. She was by now ripe for their society. Her busy, imitative mind had worked itself into many of their positions—had indeed, we suspect, occupied them with a joyous leap. *Letters and Essays*, a book whose title-page is adorned by Socrates and Burns, while Epicurus, Lavater, Rousseau, Hartley and "the excellent Dr Priestley" enrich its pages, contains some emphatic avowals of her new beliefs. "Our nature is progressive", writes this "convert to the doctrines of materialism and necessity"; and again: "The doctrine of mechanism inspires also charity and forbearance. A Necessarian may pity, but he cannot hate." It is plain, too, that she has accepted from Mary Wollstonecraft the idea that the passions in their action unfold reason; it was a useful notion to her.

Another axiom of the *Vindication*, that independence is the soil of every virtue, probably accounts for her action in leaving home and living in lodgings in Hatton Gardens. The literal interpretation is characteristic of her. Whatever small patrimony or allowance she had was eked out by literary earnings. The circle she now moved in included many writing women, Mrs Inchbald, Mrs Barbauld, Miss Alderson and others, and, helped by Dyer, she got work on the *Critical Review* and elsewhere. It was early in 1795 that she met William Godwin. She had approached him in the preceding October by writing to ask for the loan of his book, *Political Justice*, which she was anxious to read, but could not get from the libraries nor afford to buy. The philosopher, to whom the request appeared rational, lent her his book and, according to Mary, invited her to "a free disclosure of [her] opinions in the epistolary mode". One doubts whether the impulse really came from him, but he accepted the situation with kindness and discretion. She might write to him as much as she liked, but he was not to be expected to answer. He was a busy man, and a brief note or a call now and then was all he could spare. She took advantage of this concession to pour out to him the whole story of her pursuit of an unwilling man. There has been some doubt as to the identity of her quarry. Miss Wedd says that Mary withheld his name even from Godwin, but it seems unlikely that he did not know it, and Crabb Robinson is sure that it was Frend, who was by now settled in London, writing and teaching. "She confided to me on our first acquaintance that she was wretched," he writes, "the consequence of an attachment where a union was impossible.... The man whom she accused of deserting her was William Frend." And again: "Frend could not meet the love of Mary Hays with equal love....Hence desertion." Godwin himself has been proposed as the object of her affections; this Miss Wedd denies, and his appearance as Mr Francis in *Emma Courtney* does little to support the suggestion. He is there the astringent friend and monitor who opposes Emma, bewilders her and convicts her of error; and the picture reflects the slight chill that seems to have gone out from Godwin; he exercises her sensations without gratifying them, Emma says, and his manners repress even while they invite confidence. It is also to be considered that, when Godwin married Mary Wollstonecraft, Miss Hays was not one of the friends who were offended by that queer but happy union, but remained on friendly terms with them both. It is certainly possible that at some time in her headlong emotional career Godwin attracted her, but this can have been no more than a secondary affliction; the storms, the anguish, the pathetic, ridiculous obstinacy, were for another.

For the purposes of our impression of Mary Hays, however, it does not much matter who the beloved was. There was no interaction of personalities; he is seen dimly, an averted figure, through the shower of her protestations, the mists of her tears. The hero of *Emma Courtney* does not help us much. There is very little of him and what there is reminds us rather of Werther than of a Unitarian mathematician. There is no sign in either of her novels that she ever studied or understood a man. This man was the Object of her Sensibilities, but she was far more aware of them than of him. He remains then an undifferentiated Object, of whom it is difficult to predicate anything but embarrassment and a kindly temper. His humanity is evident in the final astonishing incident of this distressing affair. It had dragged on for years, but Mary had at last accepted his negative; he would not enable her to fulfil her capacities for devotion by attaching herself to him; he was deaf to the argument from social utility, and she must remain a frustrated being. She was crushed but not immobilized. Something yet remained for a philosophess to do and with considerable gallantry she undertook it. A letter to Godwin of 9 March 1796 recounts how, accompanied by a female friend, she went to call on him.

I made my friend announce and precede me to his apartment, and notwithstanding this precaution, which I conceived delicacy required, my entrance most completely disconcerted him (I had never, from motives easy to be conceived, visited him before)—
"I am come (said I smiling) to call upon you for the exercise of less

than a christian duty, the forgiveness, not of an enemy, but of a friend—I have no doubt been guilty of errors, who is free?"— I held out my hand—He took it, and replied to me, with a degree of cordiality. The past was no further alluded to.—I ask'd him, if he would, with our friend present, come and drink tea with me, to this he assented without hesitation. A few days since, they fulfilled their engagement, two other friends were also of the party. Whether he will ever think proper to call on me again, I know not, but as I conceived, *I had not been faultless*, and as it is particularly painful to me to cherish severe feelings, where I have before felt affection, I do not repent of what I have done, but feel myself relieved by it.

Mary could regard her behaviour with some complacence. It was rational and courageous; it was also extremely tenacious. William Frend would not marry her; he perhaps refused—if gossip and *Emma Courtney* are to be believed—to make her his mistress; he must then be firmly transplanted to the ground of friendship, or at worst acquaintance; somehow, at some angle, he must still be built into the fabric of her life.

Godwin's friendship and counsel were a great stay to her in this crisis. She covered vast sheets of paper to him, reporting her progress as a convalescent. Within a month of her acceptance of defeat she admits that she is better than she has been, "though certainly *very far from happy*". Her self-esteem, never a very substantial structure, had been rudely shaken. She builds it up by insisting on her superior sensitiveness, on the ardour and importance of her affections. She dreads lest Godwin should lose patience with her, and wearies him still further with insistent explanations. She explains and explains, and some of the explanations are good. "I will confess, then," she writes, "that I am not sufficiently disinterested to expect to be happy. I want a certain number of agreeable sensations for which nature has constituted me." Some of them, on the other hand, are both trivial and elaborate. She perceives fine shades of disapproval or irritation in the behaviour of her friends and hastens with anxious humility to put things right. A pointer to one of her fusses is seen in a postscript to one of Godwin's notes: "I have not the slightest suspicion of you having disgusted Mr Holcroft by interrupting the discussion on Sunday by your departure." A more notable occasion was the cold morning of 10 March 1796, the day after she had sent Godwin the letter describing her visit to Frend. She was lazily dressing by her sitting-room fire—not her usual custom as she eagerly explains—when Godwin entered the house to make an early call, and caught some glimpse of her in *négligé* as she fled across the passage— a misadventure to be laboriously accounted for in the epistolary mode the moment her toilet was complete. To Godwin she sent the first pages of *Emma Courtney*, and as she saw her novel take shape under her hands and read his guarded approval, she began to count her blessings. She was, at least, no longer convulsed by uncertainty. She could admit the balmy consolations still offered her by many gentle, benevolent spirits. She had been for a walk and enjoyed it.

I have the luxuries of cleanliness, of temperate plenty, I have moral and intellectual powers, I am free from the sting of remorse, I foster no corrosive nor malevolent passions—if there are any who have injur'd me, I wou'd return it only with kindness—And there are still some who look with an eye of tenderness on my faults, and who love my virtues—A gentle and kindly emotion swells my bosom—*I am not miserable this evening!*—How I prate to you of myself and my feelings!

The walk was perhaps in obedience to the counsels of George Dyer, given from a plane of intellectual acceptance to which she never climbed. "Pray take care of your health," he wrote to her, apparently at about this time. "Do not be a martyr to philosophy, which you will be if you do not take more exercise, be a little more foolish, and look at the world with all its awkward things, its clumsy, lumpish forms, its fools, its cockscombs, and its scoundrels, with more endurance."

The Memoirs of Emma Courtney was autobiographical to the point of including letters sent by the authoress to the "in-

flexible being"—a fact that was well-known to all her friends
and all her enemies. She must have begun to write it immediately after she had received the final repulse, for it was
published in the same year (1796). Its emotion therefore is
not recollected in tranquillity. Crabb Robinson says that the
book attracted attention as a novel of passion, but, though the
description has a meaning in its historical context, it calls up
to the modern reader comparisons that *Emma Courtney* is quite
unfitted to sustain. Aphra Behn wrote novels of passion, and
so did Charlotte Brontë, but Miss Hays's work has neither the
social poise of the one nor the lyrical intensity of the other.
She was not a real novelist. She had no invention; characters
and scenes do not live in her imagination, except as incentives
to discussion, and her dialogue speedily becomes a harangue.
When she has to devise action, it is melodramatic and un-
interesting, and, whereas it is certainly true that the subject
of the book is a woman who passionately desires the love of
a man, the exposition of that craving and of the starvation that
underlay it was by way of pedantic analysis; an analysis,
moreover, predominantly in the terms of mind, though we
need not for that reason assume that Mary Hays was unaware
of what was happening to her. The philosophers she knew
insisted on the supremacy of mind over matter, and to one
who had failed so notably to charm there must have been some
consolation in shifting her appeal on to the grounds of intellect.
Nevertheless, Crabb Robinson was doubtless right, and it was
as a novel of passion by a woman that *Emma Courtney* was
noticed. When in the second half of the eighteenth century
women had taken publicly to their pens, indulgent critics had
expressed the hope that now the world would be treated to
a picture of love from the woman's point of view. Hitherto,
however, women novelists had been too much occupied with
domestic ethics and romantic reverie, too closely bound by a
conception of delicacy that regarded the avowal of passion as
the mark of a bad, or at least an undisciplined, woman, to

carry their analysis very far. Mary Hays was one of the first to break the taboo.

Emma Courtney was written for the "feeling and thinking few" and was offered to them as an essay in philosophic fiction, a contribution, through its study of the progress of one strong, indulged passion, to the science of human nature. It would be easy to go through the book picking out the sophistries, the betraying compensations, yet the impression that is strongest as one re-reads it is that of the blundering courage and the occasional shrewdness of the author. It was by no means wholly a self-justification; the heroine's hazardous experiment in taking upon herself the initiative in love-making was meant "to operate as a *warning*, rather than as an example", and whilst there is some comfort in the thought that "it is the vigorous mind that often makes fatal mistakes", there is nothing but naked self-knowledge in Emma's cry: "Alas! my own boasted reason has been, but too often, the dupe of my imagination." It is true that Emma, marching into her confessional, carries with her something more of beauty, a greater cogency and composure of rhetoric, than belonged to her creator, even as she carries the knowledge that her love had wakened a response, a knowledge that Mary, once her girlhood was over, never enjoyed; but one cannot grudge the devotee of "utility" these few decorations.

The book has little plot, no more than is necessary to get the characters into position for the harangues, and to veil, with some slight show of decency, the conditions under which the letters were originally written. The incidents may be considered, as the author suggested, as illustrative of the workings of a distempered civilization, but this is probably not the aspect under which they will present themselves to the unprejudiced mind. The heroine, Emma Courtney, is the only daughter of a clever, dissipated man, and is brought up, happily enough, in the household of her aunt. There are touches here which pretty certainly reflect the author's girlhood. We are told of an impulsive, candid, vain, affectionate child, whose "tastes were all passions", growing up in an indulgent household, surviving with some spirit the painful shock of the transition to school life and the more painful experience of shortened means and loss of friends. In the "melancholy and oeconomical retirement" to which the family are now relegated, her solace is the circulating library, where her rate of consumption is ten to fourteen novels a week. Fiction now bestirs itself, and Emma's father, conscious that he can make no provision for her, resolves at least to strengthen her mind for her conflict with society, by introducing her to solid reading and to society where she will hear free speculative discussion. Her reading, which begins with Plutarch's *Lives*, extends to Descartes, polemic divinity and Rousseau's *Héloïse*, which charms her by "the wild career of energetic feeling". At her father's dinner table, where ladies do not have to retire before the talk becomes interesting—"a barbarous and odious custom"—she meets company that corresponds to the Godwin-Wollstonecraft circle, and collects material for reflection. Her father's death terminates this phase of her history, and the break-up of her aunt's household makes her dependent upon a hitherto unknown uncle with a harsh overbearing wife, in whose house she improves her acquaintance with the philosopher, Francis, and is sought in marriage by a young physician, Montague, whose offer she rejects. Her innocent but unorthodox conduct with Francis exposes her to the censure of her relatives, and she leaves them to go and live with Mrs Harley, a widow, in whose son Augustus she is already deeply interested. Augustus is a lawyer who has given up his profession and lives upon a legacy of £400 a year which he will lose if he marries. He lectures Emma on astronomy and philosophy from his sick-bed, but does not show himself otherwise aware of her gathering emotions, and after he has returned to London she is constrained to explain them to him in a letter beginning: "Suffer me, for a few moments, to solicit your candour and attention." The rest of the book consists largely of the letters in which she requests his affections, demonstrates why she ought to have them and systematically lays down the arguments that justify "the deviation of a solitary individual from *rules* sanctioned by usage, by prejudice, by expediency". It is a situation, she feels, that involves all her future usefulness and welfare. It is necessary for her to be esteemed and cherished. She cannot satisfy herself by venerating abstract virtue.

"Is it possible", she writes, with her emphatic punctuation, "that a mind like yours, neither hardened by prosperity nor debased by fashionable levity—which vice has not corrupted, nor ignorance brutalized—can be wholly insensible to the balmy sweetness, which natural unsophisticated affections, shed through the human heart?...I make no apologies for, because I feel no consciousness of, weakness. An attachment sanctioned by nature, reason, and virtue, ennobles the mind capable of conceiving and cherishing it: of such an attachment a corrupt heart is utterly incapable."

She meets his probable rejoinders at each point, with the adroitness of a desperate jack-in-the-box. She may be idealizing him, she admits, but her sentiments are not the less genuine, and without some degree of illusion and enthusiasm life languishes. She concludes this summons to surrender with one prudent afterthought; will he inform her if his heart is free?

In the distress of spirit that follows his polite but to her mind inconclusive reply, she pours herself out to Francis, arguing down her recurrent misgiving about an action that she would by no means recommend to general imitation. "If the affections are, indeed, generated by sympathy, where the principles, pursuits and habits are congenial—where the *end*, sought to be attained, is—

'Something than beauty dearer'

you may, perhaps, agree with me, that it is almost indifferent on which side the sentiment originates." Nevertheless:

"Those who deviate from the beaten track must expect to be entangled in thickets and wounded by many a thorn." Through these thickets she plunges, courting, one feels, the longest thorns. "In company I start and shudder from accidental allusions, in which no one but myself could trace any application." Her former frustration sharpens the edge of her anxiety. To what future, unconceived periods will the inscrutable Being who made her for an end, of which she believes herself capable, defer the satisfaction of a capacity which "like a tormenting *ignis fatuus*, has hitherto served only to torture and betray?"

From the melancholy into which she falls, in spite of Francis's philosophical ministrations, she is raised by the need of earning her living. She goes to London and begins work as a governess, and the "conscious pride of independence" does her good. Thus stimulated she writes to Harley again, admitting his right to be master of his own affections, but entreating him for an hour's frank conversation to put an end to all her doubts. "I would compose myself, listen to you, and yield to the sovereignty of reason. . . . I am exhausted by perturbation. I ask only certainty and rest." This letter extracts from him a vague reference to obligations that con-strain him, which she still refuses to consider final, and three months later she returns to the attack, begging him this time for his friendship and assuring him that she is capable of a disinterested attachment. "Why am I to deprive you of a faithful friend", she asks unexpectedly, "and myself of all the benefits I may yet derive from your conversation and kind offices? I ask, why?" For a time they meet for reading and discussion of impersonal questions, but this attempt to rise above "the prejudices that weaken human character" is defeated by Emma's unsleeping determination to extract Harley's secret from him as the only means to her peace. Under her remonstrances he becomes "captious, disputatious, gloomy and imperious", and is at last driven to admit a prior attachment. Emma, who hitherto under every repulse and coldness has resumed her pen, resumes it once more, to enforce the importance of unequivocal sincerity and to point out the harm his reserve has done her. "You have contemned a heart of no common value, you have sported with its exquisite sensibilities—but it will, still, know how to separate your virtues from your crimes." After this Parthian shot of ungenerous generosity, she ceases to see him. In her wretchedness Francis comes to her aid once more, and she survives a low fever, and sets her face to the undelightful future. But the book does not end here. Fiction allowed of a more striking conclusion than life, and Emma meets Augustus Harley twice more. The first time is at his mother's death-bed, where they have a most exhausting scene during a thunderstorm, and Emma learns that he is married and the father of two children, but cannot avow his position publicly without forfeiting his income. Years pass before she sees him again, and then, when she has long been the calm and useful wife of the physician, Montague, and the mother of a daughter, a stranger is flung from his horse passing through the town. It is, of course, Augustus. In her husband's absence she takes him in, tends him with devotion exclusive of all her other duties and receives his dying confession. He had loved her all the time. The end of the book is rather startling; Montague's jealousy, when he hears of his wife's behaviour, leads him precipitately to seduction, child-murder and suicide. Mrs Wollstonecraft felt her sympathy stop at this place, and Mrs Robinson, also a novelist, declared that the husband should have been suffered to die a natural death. Mary Hays, however, meant to trace the chain of evil effects that depends from a "confused system of morals" and a tragic personal frustration. Even at this point she does not cease to afflict her heroine. Emma devotes herself to the education of her daughter and of Augustus Harley's surviving child. At fourteen the younger Emma dies, and then the prematurely old and sad woman learns that her adopted son is involved in an unhappy love affair. For his sake, she says with almost Brontesque intensity, she has "consented to hold down, with struggling, suffocating reluctance, the loathed and bitter portion [potion?] of existence"; for his sake, to sustain him in his struggles, to impress on him the paramount importance of candour, she unseals her lips and tells him her story. By this device Mary Hays endeavoured to give an air of considered judgment and desolate calm to a book which was, in effect, an interim explosion of a permanently troublous temperament.

The parts of the narrative which diverge from the facts of autobiography need no comment; they are of a kind to explain themselves, and they are not the parts that attracted contemporary attention. Nor was it much directed to the "series of errors and mortification" which formed for Mary Hays the justification of her book, since they were intended to commend self-control; for Emma's misfortunes were quite overlooked in the glare of her deplorable enterprise. She, a female, pursued a male; not comically—at least in the author's intention—and not viciously—for even during the thunderstorm Emma calls on Augustus to acknowledge that her "wildest excesses had in them a dignified mixture of virtue" —but honourably and necessarily as an indispensable prerequisite to her social usefulness. The impressive letter, in which she "methodizes" under five heads all the objections that Augustus can possibly have to her and patiently refutes them one by one, was calculated to remain longer in the memory than her sad and humbled confession to Francis: "I am sensible, that by my extravagance, I have given a great deal of vexation (possibly some degradation) to a being, whom I had no right to persecute, or to compel to choose happiness through a medium of my creation." A clumsy forerunner of the Shavian huntress woman, humourless, charmless, and too raw and unhappy to be really formidable, she made her attack not in the name of a mystical Life-Force but of General

Utility. The mainspring of her activity, however, was not philosophic. What we see in Emma—what Mary Hays intermittently saw in herself—is the passionate temperament that seizes on the precepts of philosophy and forces them to subserve its own desires. "Philosophy, it is said, should regulate the feelings," remarks Emma, "but it has added fervor to mine." The notes of mournfulness and pride are mixed as she considers the tumult of her soul. All her life she has been a victim to the enthusiasm of her feelings, "incapable of approving or disapproving with moderation", but in this vehemence she sees a great stimulus to mental growth. "What are passions, but another name for powers? The mind capable of receiving the most forcible impressions is the sublimely improveable mind." It is with this sense of the enormous potential richness of her character that she reproaches Harley for rejecting "a mind like mine", and points out that in arresting her natural affections he is guilty of the same crime as the ascetics of monastic institutions. When she turned to philosophy, she selected instinctively those precepts that would sanction the spontaneous habits of her temperament; the candour that Mary Wollstonecraft declared to be more truly delicate than concealment, to cover the boundless communicativeness of a heart that "panted to expand its sensations"; Godwin's pronouncement that social utility is the only criterion of morals, to justify the demands of her affections for satisfaction; and his insistence on "the irresistible power of circumstances, modifying and controuling our character", to lighten her sense of responsibility. She also acknowledged with her whole heart the duty of self-examination, which can be a strict discipline but is easily deflected into an indulgence by the self-absorbed. It is to her credit as a striving human soul, "a human being loving virtue" as she pathetically insists, that she is able at times to apply these precepts, however maladroitly, to their proper end; the mists of delusion dissolve, her dreams collapse, she is self-convicted of some part of her inordinate egoism, and in floods of tears—those sudden inconvenient outbursts of weeping that are so uncomfortably lifelike in *Emma Courtney*—but with considerable courage, she retrieves her integrity and sets to work to build up her life again. Miss Hamilton was right and amusing when she set forth—she hardly needed to parody— her Bridgetina's convenient invocations of the principle of social utility. It is a phrase continually on Emma's lips. It enhances her dissatisfaction, her rebellious sense that the vigour of life in her is running to waste, her melancholy craving to "feel the value of existence" once more, by presenting to her the notion that not only she herself but society loses by her frustration. Utility is brandished as a threat in the anguished pedantry of her letters to Harley. "I have said, on this subject, you have a right to be free," she begins, with more superfluous points than usual; "but I am, now, doubtful of this right: the health of my mind being involved in the question, has rendered it a question of *utility*— and on what other basis can morals rest?" But there are times when the principle is applied without sophistication, as it is near the end of the book, where Emma clings to her denuded life in order that she may be of service to Harley's son, and writes with some fineness: "It is not to atone for past error, by cutting off the prospect of future usefulness."

The character of Emma Courtney, then, which is also the character of Mary Hays, provides in its not ignoble pretensions and its self-deluding folly the right material for comedy; and, though it is a comedy with an infusion of the grotesque—it raises loud laughter as well as soft smiling—Miss Hamilton's farcical Bridgetina, relieved against a monitory background of calamities, by no means represents it. Miss Hays did not, naturally, regard herself in a comic light; indeed, early in her life she avowed that she had "no great relish for what is termed humour". It was not by humour that she was saved from regarding her destiny as purely tragic but, once more, by philosophy. What she had to recount was a history of error and its consequences; and, since error could *ex hypothesi* be eradicated, not only would there come a time when no such history could take place, but her own individual fate was in some measure retrievable. "Let us reap from the past all the good we can," she writes in her last letter to Harley, "a close and searching knowledge of the secret springs and foldings of our own hearts." The science of morals, she believed, was not incapable of demonstration, but it required patient and laborious experiment. As such a laborious and fruitful experiment she considered her own struggles.

Miss Hays's career as a novelist may be dispatched before we pursue the career of her affections. She made one more effort, *The Victim of Prejudice*, published in 1799. In this book she aimed at a purely fictitious embodiment of the thoughts that exercised her, and the result is a crowded, melodramatic, extravagant story in which the injustice of society in punishing an involuntary lapse from chastity in the heroine is exemplified by the quite exceptional villainy of a lascivious baronet. Mary, beautiful, candid, courageous, a student of mathematics and astronomy, is a more enlightened and worse-fated Emma. Like Emma she argues her way through the book in pedantic, impassioned tirades; like Emma she is violently upset by her emotions and suffers cold shudders and burning heats. Nevertheless she is represented as a completed character, resolute and schooled in self-control. She is destroyed by the social conventions which her reason has rejected, because, as the authoress sadly remarks, while the conduct of the world is in opposition to the principles of philosophers, education will be a vain attempt. There must, in fact, be martyrs. There were moments when Miss Hays regarded herself as a martyr; but neither she nor Emma—if one can distinguish between them—were blameless in their defiance of society; their histories were avowedly examples of intellectual error. In Mary Miss Hays conceived the preparation and martyrdom of a spotless victim. It will be noted that she is never content to write of the ordinary. Beauty, malice, stupidity, wisdom and passion are always in extremes with her, and this takes all validity from her parable of the world as it is. After this book her essential literary barrenness overcame her. A letter from Southey of May 1803 shows that she had asked him to suggest subjects for a novel. He directs her attention to the use she could make of travel books for the background of an exotic story and to the studies in unusual temperaments that remain to be made; but nothing came of his advice. Her creative impulse, slight as it was, began and ended in autobiography. She sketched the face in her mirror and then, redoubling the beautifying touches of the first draft, made it the basis of an ideal portrait. After that she devoted her clumsy pen to industrious compilations, edification and a livelihood.

It is possible to find a number of reasons why she did not make her relations with Charles Lloyd the basis of a novel, of which the most obvious are the sameness of the material to that of *Emma Courtney*, a dawning sense of ridicule and the experience of savage criticism. Her abstention leaves us dependent upon the comments of the friends of both parties, but since these included Coleridge, Southey, Manning and Lamb, we may well feel more confidence in the chorus than we should have done in the monologue. The chorus is not heard, however, until the catastrophe; it does not accompany the earlier parts of the action. It was an explosion of irritation on the part of Lloyd early in 1800 that set the discussion going between his friends; but he had already been for some years the target of Mary Hays's regard. Traces of their acquaintance are plain to be seen in his novel, *Edmund Oliver*, which came out in the summer of 1798, and it may be that it is he to whom a note of Godwin's of December 1797 refers, a man whose confidence Mary Hays enjoys and by whom Godwin is instinctively repelled. As we follow these clues backwards we come very near the termination of her hopes in Frend, and perceive, as we might have expected, that her affections could not remain unfocused long.

Charles Lloyd, the son of a Quaker family of bankers in Birmingham, was fifteen years younger than Mary Hays. At twenty-two he was a delicate, nervous, self-conscious young man, and when he came to London in the late autumn of 1797 he had already several major crises behind him, and was deeply shaken in health and spirits by them. He had exchanged banking in Birmingham for the practice of poetry and philosophy with Coleridge at Nether Stowey. He had forsaken the faith of his fathers and been retrieved by Coleridge from scepticism to Christianity. In London he shared rooms with Lamb's cheerful friend, Jem White, and wrote *Edmund Oliver*, in which by an impertinent use of Coleridge's personality and life in the name-part he testified to the waning of the friendship between them. The book also testifies by the allusions to Mary Hays in the character of the anti-heroine, Lady Gertrude Sinclair, to the interest she felt in the romantic, suffering but rather unreliable young man.

Miss Hays's share in Lady Gertrude has not, I think, been hitherto noticed, and contemporary reviewers, who pounced upon the identity of her other simulacrum, Miss Bridgetina Botherim, omitted to mention this one. The allusions seem to me deliberate and unmistakable, but they do not contribute the whole outline of the figure, for Lady Gertrude, like Bridgetina, has to represent a more completely subversive mode of thought than Miss Hays ever acknowledged. She has to be an atheist, as Bridgetina was but Mary Hays never became. She has to be extremely beautiful, to add the seductions of passionate feminine charm to those of false philosophy. Moreover, since the purpose of the book is to express abhorrence at the dangerous " generalizing spirit " of Godwinite philosophy, the overleaping of specific individual duties in the name of general liberty or benevolence, she has to be brought through betrayal, despair and delirium to suicide, for which if we seek a prototype we must look beyond Mary Hays to hostile conceptions of the career of Mary Wollstonecraft. Nevertheless, in spite of these differences, Lady Gertrude's love-letter to Edward D'Oyley is in many ways so clear a pointer to the author of *Emma Courtney* that there must have been malice in the intention. Edward D'Oyley, in spite of his Quaker parents and the blurred echo in his surname, does not stand for Charles Lloyd in character, though as recipient of Lady Gertrude's letter he seems to stand temporarily in his shoes. He is the villain of the piece, the corrupter and de-stroyer of Lady Gertrude, the figment of a shocked but not a strong imagination. Lloyd's own appearance is in the shape of Charles Maurice, the staid, benign, home-and-country-loving mentor of the unstable hero—a tell-tale reversal of the original relations between himself and Coleridge.

The love-letter, in which Lady Gertrude adjures D'Oyley to spurn his Quaker parents' grovelling minds and tell them he is resolved on a connection with her, contains two acknow-ledged quotations from *Emma Courtney* and several parallels to the sentiments and arguments of that book. It is a letter in which the woman takes the initiative, claiming a return of affection on the strength of the sympathy of minds; it is vehement in tone, propping emotional appeals upon God-winite assumptions. "Promises, what are they?" asks Lady Gertrude. "Snares! fetters for the mind!...We should be decided only by the principles of the present hour." By rejecting such bonds the mind will acquire "an incredible elasticity, fitting it to the occasion". All prejudices must be destroyed and the search for truth must proceed by means of the boldest speculations and even by the collision of opposing principles, since "he who would walk erect in the difficult path of life, must often have fearlessly plunged amid the intellectual chaos; from thence he will derive stores hitherto undiscovered, and by repeating his efforts will bring new combinations from the unassimilated and unarranged elements of moral science". This is so close to Emma Courtney's letters to her adopted son, where she bids him "think freely, investigate every opinion, disdain the rust of antiquity, raise systems, invent hypotheses, and, by the absurdities they involve, seize on the clues of truth" that it can hardly be called a parody. At one point Lloyd deserts Emma Courtney to touch distinctly on the life of her creator. Lady Gertrude, like Mary Hays, deems it her duty to be perfectly sincere, and, while proposing a liaison with D'Oyley, is constrained to tell him that she "was once beloved by a youth of most interesting manners, and returned his love". This oddly pathetic and characteristically misplaced summoning of the shade of John Eccles must, one supposes, have occurred in some letter to Lloyd himself; it fits easily enough into Lady Gertrude's career, but not at all into her character; its curious air of awkward elderly maidenliness recalls Crabb Robinson's insistence that, whatever Mary Hays's principles may have been, her conduct was perfectly correct, and makes Lloyd's easy indiscretions difficult to excuse.

Outside this letter there are no demonstrable allusions, and the story soon diverges from any relation to that of Miss Hays. But the whole picture of Lady Gertrude before she is plunged into tragedy looks like the revenge of a quiet man who has been made uncomfortable, and the cause of the discomfort is spitefully underlined at the end of the book, where Edith Alwynne, the girl who is to draw Edmund Oliver out of the chaos of his sentiments and opinions into the happy discipline of domestic life, refuses to have her love for him brought, however indirectly, to his notice, since she doubts in any case of the "*propriety of a female being the first agent in these affairs*". The italics are Lloyd's; and one feels that as he wrote his gathering irritation drove him beyond his original plan. He set out to draw in Lady Gertrude, as his first pages inform us, "a woman of warm affections, strong passions, and energetic intellect, yielding herself to these loose and declamatory principles, yet at the same time uncorrupted in her intentions". Such a woman Mary Hays was; by this time, too, she has recognized, like Katisha, that she was an acquired taste, only to be appreciated by an educated palate; but when she advanced upon Charles Lloyd, prepared to take years to train him to love her, he failed to hear music in the purring of that bewildered tiger, and in feline anger scratched back. The sketch he gives of Lady Gertrude's manner, however, at the beginning of the book, seems uncoloured by spleen and entirely fulfils our expectations of what would be appropriate to Mary Hays. "Gertrude's temper was ardent—her manners earnest and impressive—she never spoke or moved but the soul beamed in her full eye.—She was impatient of control yet enthusiastic in her desires to diffuse happiness; impetuous and quick in her resentments, yet ever soliciting an admission into the stranger's breast." The last phrase is particularly revealing, and if we correct this romanticized impression by Miss Hamilton's amusing account of Bridgetina at a party, sitting "screwed up for a metaphysical argument", and seizing the first chance to launch into a premeditated harangue of second-hand materials, we get a possible picture of Mary Hays as she approached forty. Something of both versions is suggested by Southey's casual outline of her in 1797. He has met Mary Hays, he writes, "an agreeable woman and a Godwinite", who writes in the *Monthly Magazine* under the signature of M. H., "and sometimes writes nonsense there about *Helvetius*". He uses the word "nonsense" twice, but with a not unkindly inflection. Godwin talks "nonsense" about the collision of minds and Mary Hays echoes him, but he liked her well enough to dispute with her upon the moral effects of towns and maintained a friendly correspondence with her.

Whatever "nonsense" Godwin talked about the collision of minds—no doubt as a means of reaching truth—the collision of Mary's and Lloyd's was productive chiefly of perplexity and distaste in the minds of their friends. She wrote to him and, unlike Godwin, he answered, but, again unlike Godwin, with his tongue in his cheek. Coleridge calls it a "ranting, sentimental correspondence", and adds, on Lamb's authority, that Lloyd "frequently read her letters in company as a subject for *laughter*, and then sate down and answered them quite *à la Rousseau*". This was probably before he went up to Cambridge in Autumn 1798, as Manning, who became his tutor in mathematics and his friend, declares that he did not babble out her follies; but one may assume that her letters pursued him thither, and that in some fashion he continued to answer them. He had not the gentleness of Frend to a woman who was a pest; moreover, his irritation must have increased when he himself fell in love. There are contradictory statements as to the date of his marriage to Sophia Pemberton; Samuel Lloyd, in his book *The Lloyds of Birmingham*, gives it as 12 February 1799, but Lamb, writing in September to Lloyd's brother, Robert, speaks as if it were still in the future, and Mr E. V. Lucas would place it soon after the date of his letter. One suspects some connection between this marriage and the angry breach of Lloyd's relations with Mary Hays, and for this the later date would be more suitable as it was during January and February 1800 that their friends were discussing the affair; but Lloyd stayed up at Cambridge for some time after his wedding, and it is possible that it was not made public at once. At all events, whether nettled by some remonstrance of hers—she had once more cause to bewail a lack of "unequivocal sincerity"—or uneasily jesting away some touch of conscience, he first slighted her character in public and then sent her an apology, so odd and slyly barbarous that, if Lamb's version is a fair epitome of it, we must assume it to have been wrung out of Lloyd by some extreme exasperation. He had heard everywhere, he said, that she had been in love with Frend and with Godwin, and that her first novel was a transcript of her letters to Frend. Further, he had said himself that he thought she was in love with him. "In the confounding medley of ordinary conversation, I have interwoven my abhorrence of your principles with a glanced contempt for your personal character." In this fashion Sophia Pemberton's husband, soon to shake the dust of cities off his feet and retire to a pastoral solitude among the Lakes, made his apology. "My whole moral sense is up in arms against the Letter," writes Lamb. It was an added touch of ugliness in his sight that Lloyd had given it to his young sister Olivia to copy.

Mary displayed her grief and her correspondence to all her friends, to the disgust of Manning who inclined to be of Lloyd's faction. A loftily disapproving note, embracing both parties to the embroilment, is heard in a letter from Coleridge to Southey. Poor Lloyd, he remarks, is an unstable man. "Every hour new-creates him; he is his own posterity in a perpetually flowing series, and his body unfortunately retaining an external identity, *their* mutual contradictions and disagreeings are united under one name, and of course are called lies, treachery and rascality." So much for Lloyd. Of Miss Hays's intellect, he explains carefully, he thinks not *contemptuously* but certainly *despectively*, setting it lower than Southey does. "Yet I think you likely in this case to have judged better than I; for to hear a thing, ugly and petticoated, ex-syllogize a God with cold-blooded precision, and attempt to run religion through the body with an icicle, an icicle from a Scotch Hog-trough!—*I* do not endure it." The reference, I think, is to her Unitarianism—a position that Coleridge had deserted. The last word on what, so far as we know, was Mary Hays's last disappointment in love comes from a cooler Lamb, who does not go back on his judgment, but does not intend to break with Lloyd because he has faults. It comes in the shape of a proposal to Manning that one day they shall discuss "In what cases and how far sincerity is a virtue?" Not truth, he explains, "who, meaning no offence, is always ready to give an answer when she is asked why she did so and so; but a certain

forward-talking half-brother of hers, Sincerity, that am-
phibious gentleman, who is so ready to perk up his obnoxious
sentiments unasked into your notice, as Midas would his ears
into your face uncalled for." On this definition, there does
not seem much room for discussion.

During the last years of the century many things must have
combined to hurt Mary Hays. The intellectual climate
changed with the French war and grew hostile to liberalism
and to the hopes and speculations of her friends the philosophers. Mary Wollstonecraft died and Godwin, with a family
to keep, drew in his horns and walked warily. The *Anti-
Jacobin* was founded and she fell under its appalling scourge.
She had known something of adverse criticisms before, the
hectoring jollity of those blows that send the victim reeling.
The *English Review*, which had been polite to the *Cursory
Remarks*, settled the *Letters and Essays* with the observation:
"Female philosophers, while pretending to superior powers,
carry with them (such is the goodness of providence) a mental
imbecility which damns them to fame." *Emma Courtney*
received some kind words from the liberal reviews, but it was
not long before they were muzzled, and among the authors
tainted with revolutionism, whom the clerical reviewers of
the *Anti-Jacobin* haled out for public penance, Mary Hays
was not overlooked. She figured with her dear friend, Mary
Wollstonecraft, and with Ann Yearsley in the Reverend
Richard Polwhele's vicious attack, *The Unsex'd Females* (1798).
In this poem the "Arch-priestess of female Libertinism" calls
upon her sex to lay aside their winning weakness, to despise
Nature's law and aspire to blend "mental energy with Passion's
fire", and one by one, as they respond, their brows are scored
with a savage slash of the pen. Mary Hays gets off as lightly
as any one. No doubt the ineptness of the one line which
dispatches her—"And flippant Hays assum'd the cynic leer"
—in which every important word is wrong, is accounted for
by the footnote: "Mary Hays, I believe, is little known";

but this was not comforting. By May 1799 the *Anti-Jacobin* had looked her up, had found her assertion that "individuality of affection constitutes chastity", and proceeded to slaughter both her novels in a grand retrospective review, culminating in the growl: "*To your distaff, Mary.*" "As to the style of her writings," concluded the reviewer on a milder note, "it is needless to remark; who stays to admire the workmanship of a dagger wrenched from the hand of an assassin?" This was good measure, but they had not yet done with her; her private life, which indeed she had not kept private enough, remained to be exploited. Three months later they saw their chance. A harmless-looking book, John Walker's *Elements of Geography, and of Natural and Civil History*, already four years old, turned out to have been dedicated to the fair sex, whose well-wisher, the author, had rather foolishly and quite irrelevantly taken up the right of a woman to make a proposal to a man. The reviewer came down on Walker like a load of bricks. Let him ask Mary Hays. She would tell him that the "privilege of addressing" led a woman nowhere but to the loss of the "fascinating charms of female reservedness". And so forth, without any decency.

On top of these assaults came Miss Hamilton's *Memoirs of Modern Philosophers* (1800). This is an amusing and sensible book, and not unkindly. Miss Hamilton can see much to praise in Mary Wollstonecraft and in Godwin, but she mistrusts the effect of their theories on uncontrolled and undiscriminating minds, and in Mary Hays she has an example ready to her hand. To be sure, she denies that her characters are drawn from life, but this is no more than the satirist's safeguarding of his right to exaggerate, caricature and sharpen the follies of the type by the addition of the eccentricities of an individual. Reviewers, at least, had no difficulty in recognizing Mary Hays in Miss Bridgetina Botherim; all the marks were there—the short, unlovely figure, the phonographic reproduction of Godwin's philosophy, the pedantically amorous pursuit of a reluctant man. It was certainly Miss Hays, but a Miss Hays stripped of even such dignity as the *Anti-Jacobin* had left her, no more a dagger-bearing assassin, but the ridiculous aberration of a small provincial society, the comrade and dupe of shoddy "philosophic" tradesmen and rascally adventurers, as negligible as a spluttering squib against the massive good sense of the English people. The incidents that Miss Hamilton contrives, to make nonsense of her theories and sensibilities, are woundingly funny, and as Miss Hays had no capacity for fun ("I do not care for wit and humour", remarks Bridgetina, well in character) there can have been nothing to soften the impact of Miss Botherim on her mind. Apart from gratuitous humiliations, when Miss Hamilton in sheer high spirits rolls the blue and yellow finery, the stiff turban with its ribbon and the frizzled wig in the mud, she had to endure the comic perversion of her watchwords and the burlesque of her sentiment. Bridgetina quotes screeds from *Political Justice* in a small shrill voice and congratulates a friend, who has broken his arm, on the glorious opportunity he now enjoys of proving the omnipotence of mind over matter; she steeps herself in Rousseau, abandons her imagination to "the solemn sorrows of suffocating sensibility" and calls it renovating her energies. Feeling in herself "the capacity for increasing the happiness of an individual", she searches anxiously for a suitable recipient of her devotion, fixes on the local dentist, with unfortunate results, and replaces him by the young doctor, Henry Sydney, whom she addresses in inflexible love-letters that are terribly close to the original. The degree of parody is often slight; Miss Hamilton's cool hand has only to arrange side by side expressions that in *Emma Courtney* are separated, to bring out with comic force the interested and specious arguments of that heroine.

"How shall I describe my sufferings?" says Bridgetina, analysing her "importunate sensibility" to an unwilling confidante. "How shall I recount the salt, the bitter tears I shed? I yearn to be useful (cried I) but the inexpressible yearning of a soul which pants for general utility is, by the *odious institutions of a distempered civilization*, rendered abortive. O divine Philosophy! by thy light I am taught to perceive that happiness is the only true end of existence. To be happy it is necessary for me to love! Universal benevolence is an empty sound. It is individuality that sanctifies affection. But chained by the cruel fetters which unjust and detested custom has forged for my miserable and much-injured sex, I am not at liberty to go about in search of the individual whose mind would sweetly mingle with mine. Barbarous fetters! cruel chains! odious state of society! Oh, that the age of reason were but come, when no soft-souled maiden shall sigh in vain."

This is fair play enough for a satirist, though painful for the victim. Miss Hamilton, enjoying laughter, was not angry with its victim; she confined her sense of the dangers of liberal and especially non-Christian thought to another part of the book, and used Bridgetina for her sport. There is no venom in her, but her ringing cuffs must have made Miss Hays's head ache. They come most thick and fast in Bridgetina's ratiocinations over Henry Sydney's affections.

"Why should he not love me?" she demands. "What reason can he give? Do you think I have not investigated the subject? Do you think I have not examined every reason, moral and physical, that he could have against returning my passion? Do not think I have learned to philosophize for nothing."

Not for nothing, certainly, since she can put down the superior attractiveness of Julia's youthful beauty to the" unjust prejudices of an unnatural state of civilization", and see in her own surrender to her emotions "a link in the glorious chain of causation, generated in eternity". In her last letter to Sydney Miss Hamilton allows herself to enhance the colouring, while sticking close to the line of argument in *Emma Courtney*.

"You do not at present see my preferableness," admits Bridgetina, "but you may not always be blind to a truth so obvious.

How can I believe it compatible with the nature of mind, that so many strong reiterated efforts should be productive of no effect? Know, therefore, Doctor Sydney, it is my fixed purpose to persevere. I shall talk, I shall write, I shall argue, I shall pursue you; and if I have the glory of becoming a moral martyr, I shall rejoice that it is in the cause of general utility."

As a final insult, Miss Hamilton closed her spirited performance by convincing her Bridgetina of error; there is no martyrdom, but a recantation.

It is with pleasure that we contemplate the appeasing process of the years. Mary Hays had little innate faculty for peacefulness, but as time passed and wounds healed into scars, that ached only when the weather was bad, she did manage to settle down. She clung to her feminism. "I have at heart the happiness of my sex, and their advancement in the scale of national and social existence," she declares in the preface to *Female Biography* (1803), and advises her young readers to "substitute, as they fade, for the evanescent graces of youth, the more durable attractions of a cultivated mind". But she is careful to describe herself as "unconnected with any party and disdaining every species of bigotry", and she does not include Mary Wollstonecraft in her compilation. Matilda Betham, another of Lamb's acquaintances, whose *Biographical Dictionary of Celebrated Women* appeared the year after, does include her; but Miss Betham, a miniature painter, could perhaps better afford whatever risk attached to the mention of that courageous and reprobated woman than could Miss Hays, who was writing primarily for young people, and now or a little later tried her hand at teaching for a living. Still, it is an unexpected timidity, the shrinking, perhaps, of a battered fighter from another bruise.

There are very few facts to give substance to the last forty years of her long life. Miss Wedd tells us that there was at one time a suggestion, which never matured, that she should join the Southey household at Keswick; that she lived for

some time with a married brother at Wandsworth and helped
with his children—a solid family backing was to be presumed
behind her experiment in solitary housekeeping—and that she
taught for a year in a school at Oundle. The letters of Eliza
Fenwick show that by about 1811 or 1812 she was living with
her mother again, so the wanderings may have been due rather
to restlessness than necessity. She knew narrow means, but
had not to fear distress. She continued to wield her pen.
*Female Biography; or, Memoirs of Illustrious and Celebrated Women
of all ages and countries. Alphabetically arranged*, came out in
1803; it consists of six volumes of tabloid lives. At this time
she was meditating a history of manners in England from the
accession of the Stuarts, a grandiose project from which
Southey gently dissuaded her. Instead, she turned her attention to the youthful mind and produced in *Harry Clinton;
a Tale of Youth* (1804) a reworking of Brooke's *Fool of Quality*.
I have not seen this book, nor the three volumes of *Historical
Dialogues for Young Persons* which followed in 1808. They seem
to have been the fruit of her experience as schoolmistress and
aunt. From 1814 to 1824 she lived at Hot Wells, Clifton,
boarding with a Mrs Pennington, who was acquainted with
Mrs Siddons, Mrs Piozzi and Hannah More (a William
Pennington, Esq., was inducted as Master of the Ceremonies
at Hot Wells in 1785 and this may well have been his widow),
and here the fringe of Hannah More's mantle seems to have
touched her, for she became interested in one of the many
benevolent enterprises of Bristol, the Prudent Man's Friend
Society, and wrote two short tracts, *The Brothers; or Consequences.
A Story of what happens every day* (1815), and *Family Annals; or
the Sisters* (1817), to recommend it to "that most useful Part
of the Community, the Labouring Poor". The Society existed
"for the purpose of promoting provident habits and a spirit
of independence among the poor"; it acted as a bank for their
savings and made small loans to deserving cases without
charging interest. The tracts were written in simple language

and in the form of dialogues, with the scenes laid in humble life. The *Gentleman's Magazine* approved them as well-timed and sensible publications and wished that they could be introduced into the family of every labourer in the Kingdom. It is not given to many writers to be attacked by the *Anti-Jacobin* as a subversive and dangerous force and to be praised by the *Gentleman's Magazine* as a wholesome influence, to pass from discipleship to Mary Wollstonecraft to harmony with Hannah More. However, the old leaven worked in her still. Once more in her *Memoirs of Queens Illustrious and Celebrated* (1821) she lifts her voice on behalf of the moral rights and intellectual advancement of woman, and expresses her concern that the general training of her sex is rather for "the delights of the harem" than to render them the companions and counsellors of men. What, one wonders, did Miss Hays know of the delights of the harem?

This was her last book. She was then about sixty years old and speaks of herself as "declining in physical strength and mental activity", though actually she lived till 1843. Hot Wells was not her final resting-place, as it was Mrs Piozzi's and Miss More's; she came back to the Kentish edge of London, living first at Maze Hill and afterwards at Camberwell, near her girlhood's home; and since her papers were preserved with care in a sister's family, we may assume that there was domestic kindness round her in her old age.

These are scanty facts to spread over half a lifetime, not uncharacteristic but not very informative. But there is something to add that shows Mary Hays in a new and pleasing character, as a steady, wise and generous friend. These are the letters of Eliza Fenwick, written to her between 1798 and 1828, and printed by Miss Wedd in her *Fate of the Fenwicks*. It is probable that her confused and ill-disciplined but by no means poorly endowed nature had always displayed this capacity, and that her relations with her own sex had formed a background of sobriety to her extravagant designs on the other. She met

Mrs Fenwick in Mary Wollstonecraft's circle, and the two women sat together by her childbed and deathbed and remained fast friends. Mrs Fenwick, burdened with children and impeded by a shiftless husband, writes from various places in England and Ireland, and, at widening intervals, from Barbadoes and the United States. She makes Mary Hays the confidant of all her enterprises, her literary undertakings, her positions as governess, the education of her son, the launching of her daughter as an actress, the establishment of her schools in Barbadoes and on the mainland and of the lodging-house in New York. For most of her English schemes Miss Hays helped to find the money. Travelling expenses, books, and the younger Eliza's stage dresses came somehow out of her narrow income. There was always a margin for "active kindness" and a "generous loan". In 1811 Mary and Mrs Hays are taking care of the boy Lanno (Orlando) while his mother and sister are in Ireland. He was a prepossessing child, according to Mrs Fenwick, "in whom a sort of Gentlemanly temper was visible from infancy; so that it was said of him at four years old that he was born to be a plenipotentiary." Lanno—who never became a plenipotentiary, but died of fever in Barbadoes in 1816—was then in his early teens, and Mary is asked to fortify him with undeviating integrity. "Do not say that you regret that he is not your son," writes the grateful mother, "for he is yours. You are performing all the most useful, the highest, the *moral* duties of a mother." It was wise comfort, and doubtless the activity had been more comforting still; but one divines the tone of the letter that drew such an answer from busy and preoccupied Mrs Fenwick. She comments once, with an air of wonder, on the differences in their natures and fates. Eliza Fenwick, after a full and painful life, felt herself "stealing towards the grave [it was still far off and across the Atlantic] without any of those blank, lonely desolate feelings that you, dear Mary, gifted with extraordinary resources, and connected with a numerous and in a great degree kind and amiable family, too often participate". She notes with straightforward sympathy the "faithful pourtrayings of unmerited wrongs and consequent sufferings" which her friend's letters often contain. Mrs Fenwick, teaching, dressmaking, accommodating herself to incessantly changing and arduous conditions, wondered, pitied and admired; asked help and returned thanks with a simple frankness that speaks well of both parties in the process; poured forth her grief at the loss of her son, revealed at long last the unhappiness of her daughter's marriage, and in old age sent rare but warm letters of news and enquiry, breathing a hardy and not uncheerful acceptance of toil and sorrow, across a severing ocean to her "dear, prudent, considerate Friend".

To give this help and receive this acknowledgment is perhaps a small but an unassailable achievement. It is not the work of Bridgetina Botherim, nor do we find, at least in Mrs Fenwick's letters, any reference to social utility. On this ground Mary Hays was a success, and needed no philosophical terminology to make her defeat palatable; she was an effective benefactor, giving with stable benevolence to one who needed and therefore took without embarrassment. She was summoned and replied. The voice was not the voice she had hoped to hear, but it certainly enabled her to contribute to, though never to perfect, the happiness of an individual. There was no apathy in her and no silence round her; and though melancholy and restlessness may at intervals have clouded her mind, she can hardly have become sour.

NOTE ON SOURCES

The subjects and treatment of this book would make full annotation seem incongruous, but I was unwilling to send it out without indicating where I found my material, and what the difficulties are that I pass over lightly in the text.

THE POLITE MARRIAGE

The material for the study of Richard and Elizabeth Griffith was drawn almost entirely from their works, especially the *Genuine Letters*. I do not know of any modern treatment of these writers, except Professor Allardyce Nicoll's inclusion of their dramatic work in his *Eighteenth Century Drama, 1750–1800*. The *Genuine Letters* are said in a bookseller's catalogue to have been a favourite book of Robert Louis Stevenson, but I have not traced the reference. The dating of events up to and including Frances's marriage has been a difficulty. A few of the letters are dated; some—but most of these belong to the later correspondence—are datable by their allusions to such facts as the deaths of the Duke of York and the Princess Caroline; while the Griffiths's habit of recording their anniversaries is sometimes helpful. But such hints are found only in a small proportion of the correspondence, while, to darken counsel still further, the order of the letters, in spite of the corrections in the second edition, is certainly not always trustworthy. The point has some importance, as, if we accept the relative dating of the marriage and the birth of the second Richard Griffith given in the *Dictionary of National Biography*, Elizabeth Griffith must have become Richard Griffith's mistress before marriage. I have adopted the date 12 May 1751 after a careful consideration of all the indications in the letters. No single one is completely conclusive.

Contemporary references are useful to confirm facts asserted in the *Genuine Letters*, and to show that in their time they were accepted as indeed genuine. John Duncombe, prefacing the *Letters*

from Italy, in the years 1754 and 1755 (1773) of the late John, Earl
of Cork and Orrery, whose chaplain he had been, confirms Henry's
stay at Caledon, Orrery's Irish seat, in 1752, speaks of him as
"since well-known to the world as the husband and correspondent
of Frances", and gives his real name in a note. In *Select Letters
between the Late Duchess of Somerset . . .William Shenstone, Esq. and others*
(1777), edited by Thomas Hull, the actor, there is a letter from
Shenstone (vol. II, p. 132) to Hull of 26 November 1761, from
which we learn that the latter had spent months with Henry at
Kilkenny (it was probably through Hull, then at Covent Garden,
that Frances was able to essay the stage) and two from R. G-----,
Esq. (vol. II, pp. 183, 218) which have every appearance of being
Henry's own. Miss Seward's *Letters* and Fanny Burney's *Early
Diary*, on which I have drawn in my essay, agree in accepting the
letters as a picture of the Griffiths's life together, though Miss
Seward thinks it insincere, and the same point of view is taken in
notices of the book in the *Critical* and *Monthly Reviews* (May 1757,
and November 1757).

Facts about their later lives are sparse. The *Private Correspondence*
of David Garrick contains several letters from Mrs Griffith, in one
of which, dated 21 August 1777, she expresses gratitude to Heaven
and to the best of sons that her situation is easier than it has
formerly been, but wishes to assist herself "and lighten the weight
my Richard's generosity has voluntarily taken, of supporting his
family". Allusions to her career as playwright will be found in
the usual reference books, such as Baker's *Biographia Dramatica*.
Something about the scandal that attached to Richard Griffith's
last years (if we believe Miss Seward, from whom Chalmers, I
think, took his slighting remarks) might be elicited by a stricter
search of eighteenth-century magazines and newspapers than I have
been able to undertake. There are also, I believe, many autobiographical passages in their novels (e.g. the account of Andrews's
chancery suit in *The Triumvirate*, and the discovery of the secret
marriage by his father just before the birth of Fanny's son, which
results in her depression and fever after childbirth), but I have not
dared to build my narrative on these, though I have borrowed
phrases from them where the sentiments expressed ran exactly
parallel to those of the *Genuine Letters*. Richard Griffith's descent
from the ancient family of Griffith of Penrhyn, co. Caernarvon,
and his posterity down to the late Sir Richard John Waldie-

Griffith, Bart., of Hendersyde Park, Kelso, is to be found in Burke's *Peerage and Baronetage* (1931, p. 1117). I have no information about his wife's family except that she came from Glamorganshire. Richard Griffith states in the *Genuine Letters* that he has found her father's name in the list of subscribers to *Mona Antiqua Restaurata*, but I have not been able to trace the book.

Chalmers says that the *Genuine Letters* were not very successful. The subscription lists to the first and second editions, however, indicate a good deal of aristocratic and moneyed support. As for literary success, they were fairly well received, and references to them are not infrequent, especially in the novels of the period. *Letters from the Duchess de Crui* (1776; by Lady Mary Walker?) has five respectful allusions to Henry and Frances, and the author of *Arpasia: or the Wanderer* (1786) quotes what struck the fancy of women, "Mrs Griffith's amendment of the position of Rousseau, ...Rousseau in his Eloise says—to a woman who truly loves there is but one man in the world; and Frances says—to a woman who truly loves there is not a man in the world; for the object is more, and every other less." It is also not without significance that Reuss's *Register of Living Authors* gives Mrs Griffith's Christian name as Frances, and that the notice of Richard Griffith's death, in the *Gentleman's Magazine*, vol. LVIII, p. 271, shows a similar mistake, recording him as Henry Griffith, Esq.

The editions and reissues of *A Series of Genuine Letters between Henry and Frances* are a complicated subject. The first edition was published in Dublin in 1757. I have not seen this, but the priority of the Irish edition is mentioned in the notice of the English edition (v. *Monthly Review*, November 1757, p. 416, and Hull's *Select Letters*, vol. II, p. 132). The English edition was brought out by W. Johnston in the same year. It has a fifteen-page list of subscribers, is dedicated by the Editor to the Lord Bishop of Clogher, contains a letter of Henry's to the Editor and of the Editor's to the public, and has suppressed Irish place-names in favour of English ones (e.g. Conduit St. on p. 1, for Abbey St.). This last feature, to judge by Henry's remarks in the second edition, was found in the Dublin first edition as well. In 1760 appeared the *Second Edition, Revised, Corrected, Enlarged, and Improved, By the Authors. Dublin. Printed by S. Powell, in Crane-lane, for the Authors.* Mr W. Roberts, who has shown a kindly and helpful interest in the bibliographical aspects of my work, allowed me to inspect his copy of this edition. It is a presentation copy, bound in calf, and has printed in gilt inside a label on the cover of each of the two volumes, "*To Norborne Berkeley Esq' the gift of the authors*". Norborne Berkeley became Baron Botetourt in 1765 and died in 1776; the book, which comes from the library at Badminton, must have got there by means of his sister Elizabeth, wife of the fourth Duke of Beaufort. This edition has a noble list of subscribers and contains, in addition to the introductory matter of the first edition, a letter in praise of the book, reprinted from *Faulkner's Journal*, a criticism "wrote by a clergyman of taste and literature" to Henry, Frances's dedication of the second edition "*To my Sex*", replacing that to the Bishop of Clogher (which is, nevertheless, still printed) and Henry's preface to the second edition. The Irish names are restored, and some obvious misprints, mispointings and dislocations of order put right, but by no means all. The book has also been worked up a little; the authors have "supplied the chasms", as Henry says, by framing arguments out of their memories, though not to any great extent. They have also thrown in such notes, comments and allusions as occurred to them on re-reading "which would have given a pedantic stiffness to the original letters, but may help to illustrate and enliven the whole when they are submitted to the publick". Henry has also deleted some compromising references to the Bishop of Clogher's *Essay on Spirit*. Robert Clayton, Bishop of Clogher, had died in 1758 of a nervous fever, under the shadow of a prosecution, ordered by the Government in 1757 for his attacks on the Trinity. In all these respects the English second edition, printed for W. Johnston in 1761, is the counterpart of the Irish second edition. Volumes III and IV were published by Johnston in 1766, with a dedication by Henry and Frances to the Marquis of Tavistock, an address by the Editor to the Publick, and no subscription list. In 1767 the first and second volumes were reprinted by Johnston in a different type and style (there are no capital letters to the common nouns) and announced on the title-page as the *Third Edition, Revised, Corrected, Enlarged, and Improved By the Authors*. I have not detected any revisions other than those of the second edition. I should suppose the reprint was to enable Johnston to make up sets of the *Letters*; my own set is made up in this way and presents a very odd appearance. The fifth and sixth volumes were published in 1770 by Richardson and Urquhart; they are dedicated to the *Friends of the Authors* and present the same appearance as the third and fourth. In 1786 all six volumes reappear as *A New Edition. Printed (by assignment from E. Johnston) for J. Bew.* All the volumes have this title-page, but they are plainly a reissue of the sheets of the composite 1766-70 edition. There is a new, long and impressive subscription list.

There are two engraved portraits of Elizabeth Griffith in the British Museum. One, engraved by Mackenzie from a drawing by the Reverend I. Thomas, shows her in youth, with her dark hair drawn back from a high forehead, and a cap tied under her chin. She has the long straight nose that appears in the Hendersyde House portrait, pensive eyes, and thick, well-marked brows. The other is anonymous, and appeared as a plate in the *Lady's Monthly Museum*, 1801. The portrait is a half-length in an oval, while the rest of the plate is adorned with flowers, a lyre, comic and tragic masks, pens and ink, and books labelled *Del: Distress, Lady Barton, Morality of Shakespeare's Drama* and *Letters of Henry to Frances*. Here she is middle-aged, the long nose has thickened; there is a double chin and lines round the mouth, and the hair, drawn off the forehead, seems to be partly grey. Her cap, which falls in a point and is fastened to the hair with a brooch, is tied under the chin. The dark eyes look out, still pensive and expectant of hurt. The portrait is more attractive than that at Hendersyde House. She also figures as one of the *Nine Living Muses of Great Britain* in a plate, undated but assignable to the seventies, engraved by Page from a drawing by Samuel. In front of a background of pillars and landscape are ranged the female talents of the period—Angelica Kauffman, Mrs Barbauld, Miss Carter, Mrs Sheridan, Mrs Lenox, Mrs Macaulay, Miss More, Mrs Montagu and Mrs Griffith. The group seems to have been based on portraits. Mrs Griffith is not easily distinguishable among four Muses to the left of the picture. Still, she appears in good company.

I subjoin a list of the published works of Richard and Elizabeth Griffith, as the *Letters* have enabled me to add one or two books to the list in Watts's *Bibliotheca Britannica* and other reference books. It is almost certainly incomplete. Richard Griffith, at least, must have sent contributions at times to Irish and English newspapers, and there is a mysterious reference in Reuss's *Register of Living Authors* to an article by Elizabeth Griffith in the *Massachusetts Mail*. I give the date of the first publication only.

WORKS BY ELIZABETH GRIFFITH

1761. Memoirs of Ninon de l'Enclos, with her Letters.... Translated from the French by a Lady. 2 vols.
1764. Amana: a dramatic poem. By a Lady.
1765. The Platonic Wife. A Comedy. By a Lady.
1766. The Double Mistake: A Comedy.
1769. The School for Rakes: A Comedy.
1770. Memoirs, Anecdotes and Characters of the Court of Lewis XIV. Translated from Les Souvenirs or Recollections of Madame de Caylus. By the Translator of the Life and Writings of Ninon de l'Enclos.
1771. The Shipwreck and Adventures of Monsieur Pierre Viaud: Translated from the French by Mrs Griffith.
The History of Lady Barton, a novel in letters. By Mrs Griffith. 3 vols.
1772. A Wife in the Right: a comedy. By Mrs Griffith.
1775. The Morality of Shakespeare's Drama Illustrated. By Mrs Griffith.
1776. The Barber of Seville. Translated from the French.
The Story of Lady Juliana Harley. A Novel. In Letters. By Mrs Griffith. 2 vols.
1777. A Letter from Monsieur Desenfans to Mrs Montagu. Translated by Mrs Griffith.
A Collection of Novels, selected and revised by Mrs Griffith.
1780. The Times: a Comedy.
1782. Essays addressed to Young Married Women. By Mrs Griffith.

WORKS BY RICHARD GRIFFITH

1764. An Extract of the History and Genealogy of the Noble Families of the Earl and Countess of Northumberland. (Dedication signed Richard Griffith.)
The Triumvirate: or, the Authentic Memoirs of A., B., and C. 2 vols. (Preface signed Biographer Triglyph.) 2 vols.

1770. Posthumous Works of a late celebrated Genius. (A second title-page runs: The Koran: or, the Life, Character and Sentiments of Tria Juncta in Uno, M.N.A. or Master of No Arts.) 2 vols.
1772. Something New. (Preface signed Automathes.) 2 vols.
1782. Variety, a Comedy.

In 1883 *Notes and Queries* (vol. VII, p. 66) printed a set of complimentary verses by Richard Griffith to his wife, written on the fly-leaf of a copy of her *Morality of Shakespeare's Drama Illustrated*.

WORKS BY RICHARD AND ELIZABETH GRIFFITH

1757. A Series of Genuine Letters between Henry and Frances. (Vols. I, II, 1757. Vols. III, IV, 1766; vols. V, VI, 1770.)
1769. Two Novels in Letters. By the Authors of Henry and Frances. (Vols. I and II contain The Delicate Distress, by Frances; vols. III and IV The Gordian Knot, by Henry.)
1779–81. Both writers participated in a translation of Voltaire's works. Their names appear, together with those of the Reverend David Williams, Hugh Downman, M.D., J. Parry, M.A., William Campbell, LL.D. and J. Johnson, M.A., on the title-page of a volume of miscellanies (1780) and of *Annals of Empire* (1781), while Mrs Griffith alone is responsible, according to the title-page, for the four volumes of *The Spirit of Nations*, and her husband for *The Age of Louis XIV*, in three volumes, with notes. In all, fourteen volumes were published.

THE DIDACTIC LYRE

There is hardly anything to add to what has been written in the essay. The material is easily available in Downman's poems, *Essays by a Society of Gentlemen at Exeter* (Exeter: Trewman & Son, 1796), Polwhele's *Collections*, and the *Gentleman's Magazine* (vol. LXXIX, pp. 985–6, and vol. LXXX, pp. 81–4). John Downman's "stained" drawings of Hugh Downman and his wife are in the British Museum; Dr Williamson in his monograph on the painter says that he stayed with the Hugh Downmans in 1806 when he visited the West of England. The British Museum also has a presentation copy of the 1781 *Poems to Thespia*, inscribed to Mrs Siddons. Other friends of Downman might be mentioned, Isaac d'Israeli, for instance, while an acquaintance with the Griffiths is presumed by their co-operation in the translation of Voltaire; he may well have met them at Bath.

Downman is cited as a dramatist in Professor Allardyce Nicoll's *Eighteenth Century Drama, 1750–1800*. I am not aware that any attention has been paid to him as a poet since his own generation. His poetical output is less than would appear from a glance at the list of titles in the *Dictionary of National Biography* or elsewhere, owing to his habit of reprinting his poems. *The Land of the Muses*, his Spenserian imitation, first published in 1768 together with a few other poems, reappears in the 1790 *Poems* in two forms, the original stanzas and a revision in couplets, which, together with a reprint of the *Death-Song of Ragnar Lodbrach*, published separately in 1781, some of the *Thespia* elegies and one or two other sets of verses, make up the book. *Poems to Thespia* (1781) reprints the five original elegies, found in *The Land of the Muses* (1768) and adds others, while the 1791 *Poems to Thespia* reprints the 1781 volume with slight alterations, brings the number of elegies up to forty-two, adds thirty-two sonnets presented to friends with copies of the book, and fills up with complimentary verses addressed to the poet by his friends. Four new poems were added to the sixth edition of *Infancy* in 1803, and there were some accretions to the 1806 *Poems to Thespia*. To judge by the quotations in reviews, his last publication, *Poems sacred to Love and Beauty* (1809), contained at least some old work, if it did not consist entirely of it, but I have not seen the book.

THE BRISTOL MILKWOMAN

Ann Yearsley's published works are as follows:

1785. Poems, on Several Occasions. By Ann Yearsley. A Milkwoman of Bristol. (The publication was in the first week of June. The second edition is announced in Sarah Farley's *Bristol Journal* for 17 September 1785.) The advertisement in Felix Farley's *Bristol Journal*, Saturday, 25 November 1786 of the fourth edition, containing her *Narrative*, states that "the above Book has been translated into the Italian and other languages". I have no information on this point.

1787. Poems, on various subjects, by Ann Yearsley, a Milkwoman of Clifton, near Bristol. Being her Second Work.

1788. A Poem on the Inhumanity of the Slave-trade. Humbly inscribed to the Right Honourable and Right Reverend Frederick Earl of Bristol, Bishop of Derry, etc. By Ann Yearsley. (n.d. A MS. note in the B.M. copy ascribes it to 1788, which tallies with all the other indications.)

1790. Stanzas of Woe, addressed from the Heart on a Bed of Illness, to Levi Eames, Esq., Late Mayor of the City of Bristol, by Ann Yearsley, A Milk-Woman of Clifton, near Bristol.

1791. Earl Goodwin, an Historical Play. By Ann Yearsley, a Milkwoman of Clifton near Bristol.

1793. Reflections on the Death of Louis XVI. By Ann Yearsley. Bristol. Printed for, and sold by the Author, at her Public-Library, Crescent, Hotwells; and by the booksellers of Bristol, Bath, etc. (This and the following two poems are the only ones that she issued herself.)
Sequel to the Reflections. (Dated 12 February 1793. As the execution of Louis XVI was on 21 January both poems were written within three weeks. They are, however, quite short.)

1793? 1794? An Elegy on Marie Antoinette, Ci-devant Queen of France: with a Poem on the last Interview between the King of Poland and Loraski. Written by Ann Yearsley. (n.d. The Polish Partition Treaty was signed on 23 September 1793, and Marie Antoinette was executed on 16 October. To judge by the rapidity of her poetical reaction to public events in the case of the death of Louis XVI, this publication should be assigned to the end of 1793.)

1795. The Royal Captives; a Fragment of Secret History. Copied from an Old Manuscript. By Ann Yearsley. 4 vols. (Vols. I and II are noticed by the *Monthly Review* in the number for January 1795 (enlarged series, vol. XVI, pp. 112–14), vols. III and IV in that for April (vol. XVII, p. 452).)

1796. The Rural Lyre; a Volume of Poems: dedicated to The Right Honourable the Earl of Bristol, Lord Bishop of Derry. By Ann Yearsley.

The *Bristol Gazette and Public Advertiser* for 14 September 1786 has a set of verses by Ann Yearsley in answer to some by the Poetical Blacksmith of Chilcompton; on 19 October appears her satiric invocation of Dullness, and on 2 October 1787 her poem to Mrs Scrafton on the death of her daughter. On 9 August 1787 the same journal prints a bad poem in praise of Ann Yearsley by Mr Upton. I have been able to consult only odd numbers of the *Bristol Journal* and the *Public Advertiser*. Other poems by Ann Yearsley, or at least first publications of poems afterwards included in the collected volumes, must have appeared in these journals; also advertisements of her library, which I have not been able to find.

In the *Rural Lyre* she speaks of an unpublished tragedy, held back for revision. This is now lost, but may have reached the stage in Bristol, or have been available in MS., for T. D. in an essay "On the Alleged Decay of Dramatic Writings" (*Blackwood's Magazine*, June 1821, p. 281) writes: "Even Mrs Yearsley the milkwoman's tragic specimens are by no means milk and water matters." There is now only one tragic specimen available—*Earl Goodwin*. Baker, *Biog. Dram.* (vol. II, p. 182), ascribes to her a comedy *The Ode Rejected*, but adds that it is not known; this ascription has been repeated in later books of reference. Baker's evidence, however, as cited by himself, is dubious—an enigmatic allusion in an advertisement of the publication of Earl Goodwin to *The Ode Rejected* and *The Petticoat Knight*. We probably have here some comic treatment of local affairs, but not necessarily a play, or by Ann Yearsley.

An autograph letter of Ann Yearsley's, dated 29 October 1787 from Clifton, is in the British Museum (Add. MS. 18,204, fol. 196). It is addressed to an unnamed clergyman who has subscribed for her book, and is slight in substance but well phrased and written in a firm shapely hand. One notes some uncertainty as to the placing of capital letters, and the phrase: "The distance which may lay between you."

Ann Yearsley's career is referred to fairly often in the private letters and public prints of the period, and there are a few small and on the whole unimportant inconsistencies between the various references, and between them and the account transmitted by Hannah More's biographers. The most important of these, the varying descriptions of her last years and death, has been dealt with in the essay. There are also differences in the accounts of how Miss More first heard of Ann Yearsley, whether through the gentleman who succoured her in distress or through the Mores' cook. The fact that Ann Yearsley was in the habit of coming to the Mores' kitchen for the dish washings is not revealed by Miss More in her prefatory letter to Mrs Montagu, but by Ann Yearsley in her *Narrative*. Miss Edgeworth picked up a slightly different story when she was at Clifton in spring 1792 from a Miss Place, according to which Ann Cromartie washed for the Mores and it was her honesty in returning a silver spoon, rolled up in a table-cloth, that first drew Miss More's attention to the distress of the family and the daughter's genius (*v.* Maria Edgeworth, *Chosen Letters*, ed. F. V. Barry, 1931, p. 54). Finally, in the *Memoirs of Hannah More* (ed. William Roberts, 2nd ed., vol. 1, p. 352) there is a passage from a letter, dated Bristol 1784, about an unnamed recipient of her bounty, which I quote:

"Mrs Palmer, the bookseller, speaks highly of her honesty and sobriety; but says that her pride is so great, that she will let nobody know where she lodges; and it is but seldom that she can prevail upon her to eat, when she calls upon her, though she knows her at the time to be near perishing. I could not but smile at the absurd notions people entertain of right and wrong; for this preposterous pride Mrs Palmer seemed to think a noble fierté. However I have made her *condescend* to promise that, if she should have a dangerous sickness, or be confined to her bed, she would vouchsafe to let me know the place of her abode, that she might not die of want; and yet all this pride pretends to a great deal of religion. Poor creatures! not to know that humility is the foundation of virtue; and that pride is as incompatible with piety towards God, as it is with the repose of our own hearts."

This letter is not printed by Roberts with the Ann Yearsley passages, but some other letters in this chapter are also misplaced. It is taken to refer to Ann Yearsley by the author of the article in *Chambers's Journal* (*v.* below) and the picture it draws certainly has the milkwoman's air. It may have been written in the days between Miss More's return from Sandleford and her visit to Ann Yearsley's cottage in the late summer of 1784; or conceivably it may date from the beginning of the year and indicate some knowledge of her before the crisis of her misery. But surely Miss More would know where her own washerwoman lived (since Ann Yearsley's mother shared her home). We cannot combine all these versions of the story into a harmony.

A minor inconsistency concerns the performances of *Earl Goodwin*. The *Gentleman's Magazine* for November 1789 (p. 1045) reports a performance at the theatre at Bath on 2 November when the play was "very much approved", and one on 9 November at Bristol "to a highly genteel and numerous audience" and this statement is supported by John Evans in the *History of Bristol* (1816, vol. II, p. 296). On the other hand the *Bristol Gazette and Public Advertiser* (29 October 1789) announces that the first performance will take place at the Theatre Royal, Bristol, on Monday, 2 November, and on 5 November announces a repetition on the 9th. The date of Ann Yearsley's birth has been deduced from her age which was wrongly guessed by Miss More—or wrongly reported by Ann Yearsley—to be about twenty-eight in 1784. In reality she was four years older, as Clifton Church registers show. These registers also confirmed my deduction as to her maiden name, which is not elsewhere recorded, and provided information about the births of her children.

Hannah More's part in the story must be learnt chiefly from her letters, published after her death in 1833 by her biographer, William Roberts, in his *Memoirs of the Life of Miss Hannah More*. The substantial trustworthiness of these documents cannot be impugned, but Mr E. M. Forster in his *Abinger Harvest* (1936, p. 236) has reported a family tradition, not without evidence, that the editor altered Miss More's style (and consequently her sentiments and the very flavour of life as she perceived it) when he felt it unsuitable. An editor who can change "the recreant Knight of Devonshire" into "the excellent and estimable Sir T. Acland" can do anything, though it is likely that his ravages will be less severe in her solemn than in her cheerful letters: moreover the hitherto unpublished letters printed by the Reverend James Silvester in his *Hannah More. A Centenary Biography* (1934) touch on the connection with Ann Yearsley in the same tone and to the same purpose as those in the *Memoirs*. The other biographers of Miss More bring no fresh material, but there are pleasing sidelights to be found on the blue-stocking patronage of the milkwoman in Reginald Blount's *Mrs Montagu, Queen of the Blues* (1923, vol. II, pp. 134-5), where, basing his account on original material, he tells us that Miss More hired Ann Yearsley "a *little* maid", during the preparation of *Poems on Several Occasions*, and that Mrs Montagu, whom he represents as cautious and uneasy though generous,

provided her with Ossian, Dryden's *Tales* and "the most decent
of the *Metamorphoses*". It is through Mr Blount that we hear of
Ann Yearsley's gauze bonnets and other bits of defiant finery.

The reaction of the reading world to Mrs Yearsley's "genius"
and ingratitude can be gauged from Walpole's letters to Hannah
More and to the Countess of Upper Ossory between 1784 and
1787, and from Anna Seward's letters (one of which, dated
13 August 1786, appears in T. S. Whalley's *Journals and Correspondence*); less important references are to be found in Fanny
Burney's *Diary*, Mrs Delany's *Autobiography and Correspondence* (vol.
VI, p. 209), the Reverend R. Polwhele's *Reminiscences in Prose and
Verse* (1836, vol. I, p. 17) and elsewhere. The story of the Bishop
of Derry's patronage is in Nichol's *Literary Illustrations* (vol. VII,
p. 474). The best information comes naturally from Bristol. It is
a Bristol gentleman who sends the letter that the *Gentleman's
Magazine* prints in December 1784; Joseph Cottle's *Early Recol-
lections* (1837, vol. I, p. 63) are valuable, and the brief references
to her in the *History of Bristol* (vol. I by John Corry, vol. II by John
Evans) 1816, John Evans's *Picture of Bristol* (2nd ed., 1818) and the
Ponderer (1814) and in W. Matthews's *New History, Survey and
Description of Bristol* (1794) seem to be made with knowledge. The
summary of her career in Southey's *Lives and Works of Uneducated
Poets* (1831) adds nothing new, but commands our confidence, the
more as coming from a Bristol man. Lastly, in March 1856 the
Eclectic Magazine reprinted from *Chambers's Journal* (in which fertile
but trackless wilderness no doubt it could one day be found) an
article by an anonymous Bristol man, *An Historical Milkwoman*.
There is a certain confusion of details in this narrative, but I have
been able to draw from it the account of the milkwomen and their
customs and the epigram on Ann Yearsley's death. The author also
quotes on the subject a M. Lefebre Cauchy, who seems to have
written understandingly of the milkwoman, noting the absence of
love-interest in her tragedy, and observing in her *Narrative* "la
vivacité d'un bon cœur, et l'énergie d'un poète offensé". I have
not been able to trace this writer.

I know only three recent handlings of her story. Professor
Chauncey B. Tinker uses it in illustration of the eighteenth-century
idealization of the primitive and natural in *Nature's Simple Plan*
(1922, pp. 100 *et seq.*). His account, repeated from his *The Salon
and English Letters* (1915), is fair as far as it goes, but his chief

interest is not in Ann Yearsley but in her patrons. In 1925 Mr J. S. Childers, editing Southey's *Lives and Works of Uneducated Poets*, followed up the references to Ann Yearsley in the *Dictionary of National Biography* and elsewhere, and presented her life in his notes as (simultaneously or alternatively?) an "unsavoury tragedy" and a "delightful comedy". This is no improvement on Southey's judicious and sober words. Of late her career has been adequately and not unsympathetically summarized by Carl August Weber in *Bristols Bedeutung für die englische Romantik und die deutsch-englischen Beziehungen* (Studien zur englischen Philologie, vol. LXXXIX, 1935).

THE SCOTCH PARENTS

I have nothing to add on the subject of this obscure book. Even the reviews disdained to consider it. The dates are genuine (i.e. 6 November 1772 was a Thursday, as Ramble says) but this has little significance.

CLIO IN MOTLEY

Here again my material was confined to the books themselves, the reviews of them in the *Monthly* and *Critical Reviews* and the *Gentleman's Magazine* and the obituaries in the *European Magazine* for April 1799 and the *Monthly Magazine* for May 1799. There is also an obituary in the *Allgemeine Literaturzeitung. Intelligenzblatt für 1800*, S. 660. The list of his works is given in the *European Magazine* correctly, except for the omission of the pamphlet on the slave-trade, but as Watts's *Bibliotheca Britannica* and the British Museum Catalogue separate the author from the translator, I give here a complete list.

WORKS BY JAMES WHITE, ESQ.

1787. The Orations of Marcus Tullius Cicero against Caius Cornelius Verres; translated with annotations by James White, Esq.

1788. Hints for a Specific Plan for an Abolition of the Slave-Trade and for Relief of the Negroes in the British West Indies. By the Translator of Cicero's Orations against Verres.

1789. Earl Strongbow; or, The History of Richard de Clare and the Beautiful Geralda. 2 vols. (There was a French translation in the same year and a German one in 1790.)

1789. Conway Castle; a Poem. To which are added Verses to the memory of the Late Lord Chatham; and the Moon, a simile for the fashionable world. By James White, Esq.

1790. The Adventures of John of Gaunt, Duke of Lancaster. By James White, Esq., Author of Earl Strongbow, Conway Castle, etc. 3 vols. (The book appeared in German in 1791.)

1791. The Adventures of King Richard Cœur de Lion. By James White, Esq. 3 vols.

1792. Speeches of M. de Mirabeau the Elder, pronounced in the National Assembly of France. To which is prefixed a sketch of his life and character. Translated from the French edition of M. Méjan. By James White, Esq. 2 vols. (The first volume was reviewed in the *European Magazine* for March 1792, the second in the *Critical Review* for August 1792. I have seen only the first.)

1792. The History of the Revolution in France. Translated from the French of J. P. Rabaut, Member of the National Convention, by James White, Esq.

?   Letters to Lord Camden. (The obituaries alone refer to these letters; I have not been able to trace them in any review or list of pamphlets. The *European Magazine* declares that they were published and the *Annual Register* (1799, vol. II, p. 11) praises them. The *D.N.B.* dates them 1798, and Watts's *Bibliotheca Britannica* mentions *Letters to the Earl of Camden* at that date, but assigns them to Arthur O'Connor.)

Professor Wilbur L. Cross published a synopsis of *The Adventures of John of Gaunt* in *Anglia* (vol. XXV, p. 251) and mentioned him in a note to his *Development of the English Novel*. I do not know of any other modern reference before my own article "James White, Esq., a forgotten humourist", in the *Review of English Studies* (April 1927), from which I have taken a few phrases for this essay.

MARY HAYS, PHILOSOPHESS

The sources of the material for this essay are given explicitly in the text. I should like to record again my indebtedness to Miss A. F. Wedd's two books, *The Love-Letters of Mary Hays* (1925) and *The Fate of the Fenwicks* (1927) and to Mr E. V. Lucas's edition of Lamb's *Letters*. I have had to rely on a French translation of *The Victim of Prejudice*.

An enthusiastic comment on Miss Hamilton's *Memoirs of Modern Philosophers* appears on p. 199 of *Dear Miss Heber. An Eighteenth Century Correspondence*, edited by Francis Bamford (1936). Miss Iremonger, in a letter of 1 September 1800 speaks of "Miss Hamilton's superlative novel", but adds: "I feel more than half angry with her for making Rose Isted so conspicuous in *the person* and *dress* of her Heroine, tho' the professed Prototype of the *character* and *conduct* of Bridgettina is Mary Hays." I know nothing of Rose Isted.

INDEX